To Alan

Up a Hill Backwards

Best Wishes

Peter Jancaste

First published 2012 by Fast-Print Publishing of
Peterborough, England.

www.fast-print.net/store.php

Up a Hill Backwards
Copyright © Peter Lancaster 2012

ISBN: 978-178035-324-1

The right of Peter Lancaster to be identified as the author of this work has
been asserted by him in accordance with the Copyright, Designs and
Patents Act 1988 and any subsequent amendments thereto.

A catalogue record for this book is available from the British Library

An environmentally friendly book printed and bound in England by
www.printondemand-worldwide.com

This book is made entirely of chain-of-custody materials

For Joe, Les and Meg,
who are no longer with us.

About the Author

Peter Lancaster spent many years educating some of the young people of the Pennines (with varying degrees of success) finishing up as Director of Drama, at Birkdale School, in Sheffield. He is married to Jane, and they live with their daughter, Katherine, on the edge of the Peak District.

Pete was born in Manchester and brought up in Cheshire, although he is of Yorkshire stock. He is, therefore, somewhat confused about his identity and thought that writing a book might help him to discover who he really is!

Acknowledgements

I would like to thank the family of the late Peter Brook for allowing me to use an image of his painting 'Sheepdog', and also for the help I have received in this regard from Mike Baggs of 'ac gallery' (www.acgallery.co.uk). Peter came from Brighouse, as did my family, and the subject of his pictures is often a Pennine hill and a sheepdog – just like the content of this book!

I am grateful to Ian Johnson for permitting me to reproduce his image of the Rover P4 and to Martin Stuart for the photograph of South Head and Mt. Famine on the cover; also to Lancaster Brewery for allowing the picture of the pint glass.

In addition, I am indebted to various friends and colleagues for their encouragement, advice and correction. In no particular order they are: Chris Kirwan, Richard Cragg, Mike and Rosemary Amor,

Peter Riley, Mike Wilson, David Baker, Simon Bacsich, Roy Standring, Andrew Graystone, Mike Hawthorne, Paul Harper, Bob Smith, John Hassard, Peter Murray, Nancy Turner and The Poynton Writers' Guild.

Special thanks are due to Roy Chng for his technical wizardry in putting together the front cover and the map.

Finally, a thank you to my daughter, Katherine, for her help, and to my long suffering wife, Jane, for allowing me to paint a not altogether flattering picture of her – for artistic purposes!

To my Proof Readers

With Rosemary and Mike or Nancy,
You cannot write just what you fancy.
And then there's Richard, Roy and Chris,
So keen to tell you when you miss,
An umlaut or a diaeresis,
(The difference requires a thesis!)
Your pens like swords of Damocles,
Descend and put to flight my ease.
The red lines through my precious book,
(Two years it very nearly took!)
Is it a colon or a dash?
I see that I have made a hash.
'Avaunt, you double negatives,
'Begone, all split infinitives'.
Until the text's correct and gleaming,
So effortless and lovely seeming,
Black and beautiful on white,
The page a pedant's pure delight.
So, thank you to my fine schoolmasters,
For stopping some complete disasters!

Contents

– UP A HILL BACKWARDS –

Peter Lancaster

An Introduction to the Pennines

'If you don't scale the mountain, you can't view the plain.'
- Chinese Proverb

The word 'Pennine' probably originated with the Romans, who named this range of hills after The 'Apennines' in Italy. The Apennines, like the Pennine Chain in Northern England, form a spine or 'backbone' to the 'body' of Italy. However, whether you call them 'The Pennines', 'The Backbone of England', 'The Penny Chain', or even, as I have heard them described, 'The Silly Bugger Hills', the names all refer to the same thing - those great lumps of limestone, shale and millstone grit, raised from the seabed by the collision of ancient continents and sculpted over aeons by the action of water and ice, which squat over the North of England. They are also the first proper peaks you encounter travelling north from London!

The Pennines rise around and about Ashbourne in South Derbyshire, and continue northwards as far as the Scottish border, where they spit out into the North Sea at Lindisfarne. Generally, they are between thirty and fifty miles across, but halfway up they spread east and west briefly, so that the overall impression from a map or from space is of a cruciform shape. In the west this crosspiece is completed by the Lake District and in the east by the North York Moors. Strictly, they are not part of the Pennines but to me they are connected intimately, and I have included them in my rambles.

Over millennia men have farmed, mined, built on and warred over the Pennines; they have enjoyed and endured them in all of their changing moods. They were the crucible from which steel was forged, coal mined and wood hewn, in order to build the ships that ruled the waves. Out of these moors and dales sprang Captain James Cook, Richard Arkwright and George Stephenson, men who took the raw materials of their native hills and made Britain great. From here also came Ant and Dec and most of Girls Aloud. Hmmm!

Can there be a more fitting touchstone for the state of our health than the Pennines? Where better to revive our flagging spirits but on the cross of these mighty peaks? When things are an uphill struggle let's pause to take breath and look at the view. Let's follow in the footsteps of the heroes of old, and head for the hills!

Route map

Prologue
The Vikings

It is 1961. A small boy sits in a Vanguard, the latest car in the Standard range, in the car park of 'The Leigh Arms', near Alderley Edge in Cheshire. It is quite a posh area and it is generally held that his father has 'done well for himself', living as they do in a detached house. It is due to his dad's job that the boy was born in Cheshire and not Yorkshire, away from the rest of his extended family, and so consequently he is growing up alone, a Yorkshireman in exile, unable to play cricket for the county, or even understand his relatives.

The boy is holding a bottle of tomato juice with a straw in it and picking carefully at the last salty scraps in the bottom of a Smiths Crisps packet. His parents are in the nearby pub and come out occasionally to see how he is doing, as children are not allowed in pubs.

The little boy is 'doing alright'. He is not unhappy; he feels safe, if a tiny bit bored. In the pub his parents are talking to his Uncle Reggie, who has come to visit with Grandma. He has driven over on a motor-bike, carrying Grandma in a side-car. She looks identical to the cartoon 'Grandma' created by Giles, as once seen in 'The Daily Express', complete with long, black overcoat, fox fur and a battered bonnet.

She lives in a 'one-up and one-down' back-to-back house with an outside toilet and, because she is normally short of company, she never stops talking. She regales us with stories about when the Salvation Army were chased out of town or about why she throws tea leaves over any car that dares to park in front of her house.

Uncle Reggie is a miner at a clay pit in Brighouse. On the way back to the boy's uneventful home he talks loudly in a broad Yorkshire accent about how the miners have to defecate onto their shovels if they need the toilet. I don't think he used the word defecate, but fortunately his accent is so thick that the boy can hardly understand a word his uncle says.

Later, at home in his bedroom, the young boy turns off the central heating radiator, climbs quietly into his clean double-bed, in his freshly decorated modern room, and listens to the adults below. They are talking loudly about things that seem a world away from his experience. They belonged to the generation that had lived through the war, and who had endured some tough times. They had really lived these people, really touched some bedrock of human experience, whereas we 'baby-boomers' had simply 'never had it so good'. We lived in Wordsworth Close or Coleridge Crescent, in 'little boxes made of ticky-tacky' that 'all look just the same'; an endless suburban wilderness repeated up and down the land forever and ever, amen.

The boy isn't able to articulate this of course, he just feels vaguely uneasy. Out of his bedroom window he can see, in the far distance, the hills where his family comes from, and a sense of longing overcomes him.

★ ★ ★

It is 1975, and the boy, now a young man, sits at a grand dining table at his girl-friend's house in Southgate, North London. The young man likes London. It feels like an important place, but it is busy...so busy. There is little chance of any stillness, no opportunity for reflection, and there are no views from a hilltop.

At the dinner table conversation is rarefied, if not non-existent, and whilst the head of the house stands silently carving the meat, everybody looks stiffly at each other. Eventually, Grandmother, an elegant yet rather forbidding lady, turns to the young man to ask,

"And where do *you* come from?"

The young man is startled and through his panicking brain runs a series of locations that he might use for an answer, spinning like the columns on a fruit machine. The lever on the fruit machine stops with a clunk, and the words

"The Pennines" pop out of his mouth, followed by a simper.

The forbidding old lady raises her eyebrows.

"Oh, you come from *up there* do you?"

The words hang in the air a moment before settling like frost on the table, and the young man feels as though it might be better for him to return to the woodwork from whence he has obviously crawled. He thinks to himself,

'Up there, up where? Who am I anyway?'

A little later the young man gets into his old Rover car, the one with the Viking bonnet badge, and heads north.

The relationship didn't last.

Chapter 1
Travels with 'Auntie'

"Jane, have you seen my lump hammer?"

It was an innocent enough question and, in my opinion, deserved better than the response it received. My wife looked up suspiciously from the pile of supplies now threatening to engulf her in our kitchen.

"Are you trying to be funny, Pete - or fresh? If not, then *why* would I have your lump hammer? Do you imagine it is on my list of things to pack? And incidentally, why do we need a lump hammer on holiday?"

"Well," I responded, in an aggrieved tone, "if 'Auntie' has a puncture I need it to loosen the nuts."

"Puncture, flat battery, faulty fuel-pump!" continued my wife, now all but invisible under the mountain of stuff that was to accompany us on our trip through the Pennines. "When are we going to get a modern car?"

Now, you can insult me as much as you like and I will just shrug it off, but criticise my 1963 classic Rover motor car and I am wounded. I have had her for over thirty years and she is part of the family. The Rover P4 is two tons of battleship and luxury liner and her nickname is 'Auntie'. I suppose she has earned this name because she cossets you, like a kindly maiden aunt. Her interior consists of acres of shiny leather and wood, and her mighty leaf springs turn a ride over a rough road into a symphony of peace and harmony.

I adopted the expression of an unfairly abused, yet kindly, martyr and prepared to make a grand exit, before I remembered that it was our Silver Wedding Anniversary, and that Jane and I were supposed to be celebrating. We were taking a nostalgic ramble over the Pennine hills – those moors and dales that erupt south of Ashbourne in Derbyshire, and travel north as far as Northumberland. We also planned to take in the North York Moors and the Lake District, just for good measure.

Such an odyssey demands meticulous planning and my normally easy-going partner had transformed into an SS Gruppenführer, flinging out orders and garnering the most obscure bits of kit. I regarded the swaying heap and mentally picked out various sundry items, such as a cruet set. Why would we need that when we weren't self catering? And was that a lemon squeezer? A lump hammer seemed relatively useful by comparison.

"Just in case!" glowered Jane, following my line of vision.

"Well," I grumbled, petulantly, "I suppose if we get stuck up a mountain then we can enjoy lightly-salted lemon juice."

I retreated before said squeezer flew past my ear.

I headed out onto the drive to make sure that 'Auntie' was suitably buffed and ready for the shortly arriving mule train; it is just as well she is large and sturdy. 'Auntie' has accompanied me on many a journey along the Pennine Chain. When I get sick of the 'rat race' I jump behind the wheel and take to the road, and the hills. With the valve radio tuned to Radio 4, I grip the enormous steering wheel and relax into the armchair-like driving seat provided by the Rover Car Company.

Anyway, the hills always put life into perspective for me. They are so majestic and unchanging that I return home refreshed, feeling that perhaps things aren't so bad after all. A kind of magic emanates from the landscape which lifts and inspires me. Things past whisper out of the mouth of Pennine caves. Standing Stones speak of battles fought long ago, or of rituals performed on hill tops to a rising sun. Is this why, in my dreams, I am running naked through some endless moorland landscape, with the wind rushing past my face and heather tickling me elsewheres? I had always put it down to eating cheese before going to bed.

I suppose (being our Silver Wedding) Jane and I could have gone somewhere more exotic, or at least warmer, but the Pennines have always held a particular affection for us. I had been brought up on the plains of Cheshire, but Jane was a 'hill girl' from the Peak District. All my life I had raised my eyes to the hills with expectation, so imagine my delight one day when I saw this vision of loveliness called Jane, running down a hill, singing 'The Hills are Alive' from 'The Sound of Music'. I was smitten! The hillside burst into song all around me; flowers bloomed, lambs skipped, and were those wedding bells chiming in my head?

Courting Jane involved driving 'Auntie' from the lowlands of Cheshire to the heights of Derbyshire.

Often, when it was merely raining round our way, it would be snowing hard on the peaks. Once, just as I was congratulating myself for having made it to the foot of the slope where Jane lived, my poor old car skidded and slammed into a stone wall. Fortunately, 'Auntie' is made of stern stuff, but I took it as a sign. I had to find out more about these hills, for one thing to avoid crashing all over them. They were a revelation to me; I felt like I was returning to my roots.

After several years Jane finally agreed to take me on. In the intervening time I had researched the area pretty well. I knew that Jane's surname (Kirk) was a Viking name and that the Pennines had once been settled by the Vikings. Perhaps I had Viking ancestry as well? Of course, the Vikings roved all over the place, but they were content to stay in these northern hills for centuries, beating their swords into ploughshares.

Coincidentally, in the middle of the steering wheel on 'Auntie' the image of a Viking warrior stares back at you; this is the horn. A similar effigy in chrome sits at the end of the bonnet, surmounting the radiator. Since 1904, the Viking has been the symbol of the Rover Car Company; and what better companion could you wish for on a journey through the wilderness than an aunt, who happens to be a steely Viking?

My ruminations were interrupted by the appearance of our sheepdog, Meg. Never one to stand on ceremony, she jumped straight on to the back seat and settled down. She knew, like all dogs seem to do, that we were going away – and she was determined not to be left out. Meg is a good traveller and only creates alarm when she senses that she is close to somewhere familiar. She will then employ a piercing, squeaky bark until everybody has chorused "Shut up!" loudly and frequently. However, Meg's appearance was a good omen because it meant that Jane was ready for me to load up 'Auntie'. Meg needed to be in the car first so that I could pack things round her.

Soon, we were stuffed to the gills and ready to roll, with Meg peeping at us from behind a pile of boxes. I was determined to do this trip properly, starting at the very foot of the Pennines. Our intention was to revisit all those places that had meant something special to us throughout our marriage. We had lived and worked in the Pennines for most of that time, Jane as a Careers Adviser and me as a teacher. Also we loved the Lake District and the North York Moors.

So it was in a state of high excitement that we set off, marred only by the nagging doubt, common to all travellers, that we had forgotten something. It promised to be a great adventure. If only we had known that before the day was over we would be murdered – almost.

Chapter 2
'Auntie' Escapes the Raiding Party

'I raise my eyes unto the hills…'

Three hundred and sixty-four days out of three hundred and sixty-five Ashbourne is a sleepy little town. Situated at the foot of the Pennines, on the old road from London to Manchester, it is a centre for both hill dwellers to the north and plain dwellers to the south. They come for the market, the rather swish shops, and a 'mooch' around the cobbled square with its many listed buildings. There was never much industry in Ashbourne. It makes its way in life serving the needs of the local community, based on brewing, tanning and food produce. It is sleepy, refined and comfortable - for three hundred and sixty-four days of the year.

Unfortunately we had arrived on day number three hundred and sixty-five. Our plan was to stay near Ashbourne before heading north towards Leek and Buxton. From there we would travel east to Chatsworth, Chesterfield and Sheffield, before heading west to Cheshire and Greater Manchester. If we had any energy left we would then travel north through the Trough of Bowland, southeast to Haworth and Brighouse and then northeast to Harrogate and Whitby. The final push would be up to Durham and Northumberland, before descending gently southwest to the Lake District. I hoped that 'Auntie' was up to the task, but there was a more pressing problem – it seemed likely that we were going to die!

Stopping at some traffic lights I noticed a youth suddenly vault from behind a nearby wall and then lurch into the street, looking back over his shoulder. He was followed by another and then another. Soon there were dozens of clearly exercised and impassioned young men all milling about on the pavement next to our car.

Now this is not so unusual an experience for me because 'Auntie' invites admiration. She comes complete with proper wing-mirrors, quarter-lights and lots of chrome work, which people do like to gaze fondly upon. If you still can't picture her she is the model featured at the beginning of the TV series 'All

Creatures Great and Small', being driven through a ford by Siegfried Farnon. However, this amount of attention was somewhat excessive. I waved shyly at the wildly staring young men and smiled sweetly. Craning my neck I peered over the wall and was alarmed to see hundreds of sweaty and angry looking people charging in our direction. Had anarchy broken out in the town or was it some sort of coup?

The dog was no use; instead of guarding us she just burrowed deeper into the pile of stuff that surrounded her. It looked like it was 'curtains'. I turned to Jane, and started to mumble inadequate goodbyes.

"Stop being silly," she interjected. "Don't you know what day it is?"

"It's Tuesday isn't it?" I ventured tentatively.

"It's *Shrove* Tuesday!"

"Of course it is! Oh well, I'll whip-up some pancake batter and everything will be alright!"

Jane sighed. "Don't you remember the famous Ashbourne Shrovetide Football Match?"

"Football Match? It's more like a scene out of 'Braveheart'!"

I slapped my forehead with the palm of my hand in frustration. What a time and a place to pick for the start of our exploration of the Pennines. This was meant to be an anniversary treat to discover wonderful places and people, and here we were being pillaged by the natives. Up to this point we had had a pleasant and relaxing journey heading north out of the West Midlands. There is definitely a sense of freedom to be had as you travel up-country from the great conurbations of Birmingham and Coventry. The aspect opens up, making it feel like there is 'room to breathe', and there is a general relaxation of tension in the air, allowing you to notice things like the existence of birds and trees. The traffic begins to subside and the flat lands of Staffordshire and South Derbyshire give way to gently rolling hills. The road sails up and down as if it is heading into a rising Atlantic swell.

'Surely this is what life is all about', I thought to myself as I regarded the pretty landscapes. My cares and worries began to fade away and I became mellow, happy even, and charitable. I smiled benignly at Jane, glad of her company in this journey of reminiscence and discovery.

I was brought back to the present, forcibly, by a loud roaring noise, accompanied by the shocking appearance of a great crowd of men. They were all pulling and tugging at something that might once have been a football, milling about in front of the car like a colony of ants fussing around the queen. They moved first one way and then the other, in a seemingly purposeless melee. We were slap-bang in the middle of the Shrovetide Football Match!

The origins of this strange 'game' are buried in the mists of time but basically it seems to involve the residents of the town who live north of the river (the 'Up-ards') taking on those who live south of the river (the 'Down-ards') in what appears to be a cross between rugby and murder. A ball is thrown in the air by some local dignitary outside 'The Green Man and Black's Head', but not before suitable amounts of beer have been consumed, and stirring verses sung recounting death and disaster from previous matches. Hundreds of people then try and grab the ball to take it to some fixed point north or south of the river. It takes hours, or even days, but it all seems *fairly* amicable, and now has 'Royal' as a prefix, having been kicked off on occasion by both Edward VIII and the current Prince of Wales.

Nevertheless this wasn't the time to hang around so I floored the accelerator on 'Auntie' and she rocketed forward - at almost ten miles per hour - belching a great cloud of smoke from the exhaust. This proved handy in facilitating our escape from the baying mob and we managed to make it to the town square where we paused for breath. You see, 'Auntie' is not used to such rough treatment. She normally proceeds down the road sedately with her engine purring. The only other noise you expect to hear is a soft tick from the 'Longines' clock in the centre of the highly-polished dashboard.

We glanced around the normally bustling market place but it was deserted. The shop windows were boarded up and the stalls had disappeared. Only the odd person could be seen peering nervously out of a pub doorway. I felt like Gary Cooper in 'High Noon'.

The absence of people gave us a good opportunity to note the more unusual listed 'objects' in the town. There are not only listed buildings in Ashbourne. The cobbled pavement is listed, as is a telephone kiosk, a lamppost, and the railings to the park. Even the pub sign of 'The Green Man and Black's Head' is a listed object!

This great pub used to be two separate, semi-detached pubs but at some stage (nobody seems to know quite when) they joined together. Not only did the buildings join but so did the names. Its full title now provides the longest pub name in the world, namely 'The Royal Green Man and Blackamoor's Head Commercial and Family Hotel'. In the middle of the 18th century Samuel Johnson was a frequent customer and the pub is mentioned in Boswell's 'Life of Johnson', recounting how the great lexicographer and Boswell ate here when visiting friends in Ashbourne. You can still get a pint of 'Samuel Johnson Ale', although today I was prepared to pass!

Ashbourne prospered under the influence of Cockayne. This is not as bad as it sounds because Cockayne was the surname of the family who were granted lands in this area in the 12th century. In Old English this strange name means 'cockerel people', or 'people who live with cocks'. More hopefully, it is of medieval French origin, Cockayne being a mythical land of idleness and plenty, from where (in part) we get the modern name for the drug. I noted several pubs around the market place but they had all resisted the temptation to call themselves 'The Cockayne Arms'.

The Cockaynes arrived in England with William the Conqueror, in 1066, and as a reward for supporting him they received estates which had previously belonged to Anglo-Saxons (a case of 'to the victor the spoils'). Once installed they were free to use the natives as they liked, and the odd foray round the local hovels to slaughter a few Saxons most likely kept them in their place.

However, from where we were parked I could see evidence of the Cockaynes' later and more constructive handiwork. They built Ashbourne Hall and St Oswald's Church, which stand west and east of the town respectively. Ashbourne Hall has had a chequered history, being partially demolished in the 18th century and rebuilt in the Georgian style. What is now the Memorial Park used to be the grounds of the hall.

St Oswald's Church is named after the seventh century Northumbrian king and saint, and is worth a visit. It is a huge building, more on the scale of a cathedral, with a spire so high, at 212 feet, that no less a figure than George Eliot was moved to describe it as 'the finest spire in England'.

The interior boasts a stained-glass window depicting the coat of arms of the Cockayne family, and contains the tombs of several prominent Cockaynes, such as Sir John Cockayne who was steward to John of Gaunt, and Sir Thomas Cockayne, 'The Magnificent'.

The latter was given this soubriquet by Henry VIII in recognition of his brave deeds at the Battle of Tournai in 1513. Other notable Cockaynes include the splendidly named Sir Reginald Cockayne-Cockayne and Caleb Cockayne, who subsequently lost the family fortune. More information about the entertaining Cockaynes and their legacy can be found in a booklet by local historian George Shaw, entitled, somewhat ambiguously, 'From Cockayne to the Queen'.

Ashbourne sits below an area known as The White Peak. Farms and houses round about are made of local stone which is a feature common to all Pennine regions. Perhaps this has had some influence on the character of the people who live here. All that hewing of stone and heaving it up hill and down dale, before chiselling it into blocks, must make one pretty resilient, and probably too exhausted for social niceties. It has produced men of few words, who can make 'ay-up' mean so many different things! The Cockaynes must have found them frustrating.

Although it might have been nice to get out of the car and wander around on day three hundred and sixty-five, we judged it not to be the best time for window-shopping so, managing to escape the worst excesses of the celebrations, we pressed on, northwards. Up to this point the hills arise rather coyly from the plain, showing a great sense of domesticity and decorum. But hereon in they become seriously high, angular and sharp, with an air that commands both awe and respect. 'We are not to be trifled with' is the message they convey. In the sunlight the knife-edges of stone cast jagged outlines on the hillsides and clouds chase their shadows closely along the endless dry stone walls. It has been said that there are no real peaks in the Peak District but this is not quite true. The hills round about here are definitely pointy!

It is the action of rainwater on limestone that creates the sharp edges and the steep sided valleys of this region, a process started aeons ago, yet continuing gently every day. Alluvial deposits in the valley bottoms make for fertile and tree-lined fields and rivers flow dramatically down from rocky outcrops in the form of throaty waterfalls. Northwest of Ashbourne can be found the great shoulder of Thorpe Cloud, and the columns of the 'Twelve Apostles', which stand sentinel over gorgeous Dovedale.

Here also man has made his impact on the country. Ilam Hall stands at one end of Dovedale and 'The Izaac Walton Hotel' stands at the other. The hotel is named after the man who did so much to popularise fishing in England with his book 'The Compleat Angler', written in 1653. The area of Ashbourne and Hartington feature prominently in the book and Walton's fishing lodge on the River Dove is still in existence.

Here was the first real test for the car as it is a steep climb out of Ashbourne. We were reduced to the whining first gear occasionally and the thought that if it proved to be still too high a gear then we would probably be reduced to reversing uphill. However, the old girl handled it well and, with memories of the raiding party fading, we began to pass through some lovely villages, like Fenny Bentley and Tissington. We decided to pull over at the popular centre of Hartington in the Manifold Valley, because we wanted to revisit a lovely hill nearby, called Ecton. From the top you get a 360 degree view of the whole of the White Peak and you can trace the course of the rivers through the Manifold Valley.

This valley really is a sublime bit of the Creation, despite the fact that its name sounds like part of a car engine. The River Dove and the River Manifold run through its centre and they have many branches and tributaries, passing along dales such as Wolfscote Dale and Narrowdale. As its name suggests Narrowdale is breadth-ly challenged, giving rise to the saying 'As Late as a Narrowdale Noon'. Knowing that there is a small brewery nearby I suppose you could change the saying to 'As Pissed as a Narrowdale Newt'!

Another interesting feature on Ecton is the spoil heap of a former copper mine. This doesn't sound very attractive but when you realise that the workings consist of a sparkling fluorspar rock then it becomes quite magical - a veritable crystal mountain. When our daughter was young her grandad often took her to 'Crystal Mountain', to collect shiny bits of stone. After a while she had so many bags of rocks under her bed that we considered strengthening the floorboards in the bedroom.

What we didn't know at the time of our current trip was that since our last visit 'Crystal Mountain' had become an SSSI, or Site of Special Scientific Interest. There was no sign to say so and we only found out by accident. For old times sake we were rummaging through piles of fluorspar when a rather officious looking chap approached us. Did we know that this was an SSSI and that disturbing of the site was not allowed, still less collecting crystals? He had with him a group of geology students he said, indicating a little huddle of cagoules that we hadn't noticed. He was allowing them to carefully remove a few grains of crystals. They were crouching down in a line and, one by one, they would edge forward gingerly, holding a pair of tweezers and a brush in gloved hands. When they reached the spot appointed by the official they would lie on the floor and sweep a crumb of material towards their tweezers. Picking up this minuscule specimen they then retreated to neutral territory, allowing the next student to reverently approach 'The Holy Grail'.

And here were we trampling all over the place! I started to protest that we were doing no real harm when our dog, which never normally bothers with such things, suddenly started to dig frantically on the ground, launching crystals of special scientific interest in every direction. It sort of ruined my argument and so we had to give way on that point. If anyone wants a bag or two of crystal rocks, I've got plenty.

The last great magical treat to be found on Ecton Hill is mushrooms. My father-in-law got me into picking mushrooms, and Ecton is awash with them in season. You can find Field Mushrooms, Horse Mushrooms, Puffballs and Shaggy Ink Caps, all of which are edible. You have to know what you are picking though as there are some pretty deadly varieties of fungus out there, such as the Destroying Angel or the Fly Agaric. There is no hard and fast rule with fungi but generally the red ones are bad; having said that the Destroying Angel is white all over. If you eat one you will soon be violently sick and get terrible stomach cramps. You will then seem to recover, no doubt grateful to be alive, but after about three weeks you suddenly drop dead in your tracks!

The Fly Agaric is a big red fungus with white spots all over it. Like the Destroying Angel it is also poisonous, and will cause retching and possible damage to internal organs but, if you can get past that, then the psychotropic compounds within begin to work on your mind. The ancient Celts ate all sorts of fungi but apparently only the druids were allowed to have the Fly Agaric, to facilitate the exploration of the mind. No wonder they saw fairies sitting on the tops of toadstools. This mind-bending fungus is supposed to be a favourite of Siberian Reindeer. After eating it they go slightly loopy and jump around a lot, reputedly giving rise to the legend of Santa's flying sleigh. I am guessing that the reindeer handlers had probably been partaking as well to arrive at such an explanation of events.

A charming toadstool to look out for is the Stinkhorn or, to give it its Latin name, Phallus Impudicus, which smells of rotting meat and looks like a giant penis. We had one of these growing outside our house once and it became a real talking point in the neighbourhood! Another one to avoid is the hallucinogenic 'Magic Mushroom', which I often find growing in the park near where we live. Come autumn time you find a steady stream of hooded young men taking an unaccustomed stroll through the countryside. At first I thought the 'chavvy' chaps had seen the error of their ways and were trying to commune with nature, until I realised what they were after. If you believe that this is a new phenomenon then think again. A friend of mine, who has written extensively about the 10th century Vikings, told me that they used to get high on 'Magic Mushrooms' before going into battle.

After our brush with death in Ashbourne I felt the need to stiffen my sinews, not with any fungus but with a pint. You have to drive round the foot of Ecton Hill to get to the local brewery. Then you take a very minor road out of Hartington: so minor, in fact, that it has grass growing in the centre of it. Fortunately 'Auntie' has good ground clearance and we took our chances. The lane soon became a track, then something more like a footpath, and then it forked several times, each fork being indistinguishable from the others. It went on like this for miles and I began to lose confidence, as did Jane who let me know in no uncertain terms. If an old map for the area were to be found I am certain that it would say 'Here be Dragons'. It was so completely deserted that I started to wonder, in the event of any mishap, whether my affairs were in order.

Just as we had lost hope and I was preparing to make a goodbye speech for the second time that day, what appeared to be an abandoned farm hove into view. It was perched on a promontory overlooking a steep gorge and looked as if it had been left in a hurry some time ago. There were broken gates, rusting tractors and other farm implements, all lying around like some sort of agricultural 'Marie Celeste'. The only clue to its current purpose lay in a stack of battered beer barrels of various sizes, teetering amongst nettles and weeds by the side of a barn.

We approached cautiously and parked up. Sadly, Jane is not as keen on beer as I am so she stayed in the car whilst I got out to investigate.

Immediately, a deep thrumming, humming noise assaulted my ears, coming from the direction of the barn. It was steady, persistent and rather ominous to my mind. Now, I am not given to flights of fancy but with nerves a tad frayed after the events of the day, my imagination began to play tricks. What better place for the government to plan the recapture of Ashbourne than from this close yet isolated location? Worse, suppose alien investigations of the weird activities observed in the town were taking place in this seemingly innocent-looking dilapidated building? Any second now I might be drawn in by some tractor beam and probed in unspeakable places by unearthly entities, in order to establish my northern identity. I was in a complete funk. The tune from the X-Files began to run through my head.

The next moment, to my immense relief, there descended on the nose a beautiful floral aroma - the fermenting of hops. What a soothing scent that is. What a balm to the over-heated brain! I knocked on the door of the barn but hearing no response I lifted the latch and pushed it open. The smell became overpowering and the humming noise intense. There, in the middle of this small scruffy hay-barn, were three enormous stainless-steel containers or tuns, each one designed to fulfil a part of the brewing process. What's more I had it to all to myself; there was not a soul in sight. I wrestled with the temptation to shout 'Goodbye cruel world' and dive in. What a way to go!

Resisting sin, however, I walked through to the other side of the barn and came out by some steps from where there was a lovely view of Wolfscote Dale below, with the village of Alstonefield in the far distance. Suddenly, a baying of hounds broke out and it was obvious that I had been spotted. A lady stuck her head out of a door above, smiled at me and asked,

"Have you come for the tour?"

Before I could answer there was a noise of tyres on gravel and a minibus turned the corner into the yard. Out poured a chattering group of what I presumed were tourists, speaking in not one but several different languages, none of them English. It was a bizarre sound, as if this time and place had been chosen for a modern revival of the Day of Pentecost.

Quickly, they gathered into their language groups with their guides and translators. Improbably, they were a party of Russians and a party of Italians, as well as one or two British. I decided to tag along as the nice lady from the brewery began showing people around. This promised to be a very short tour as it was a very small brewery. Once we had talked about the ingredients of beer - hops, malted barley and yeast, then looked at the three tuns - the hot-water tun, the mash tun and the fermenting tun, it was straight on to the sampling.

In truth, the sampling lasted a lot longer than one would have expected, because of the twin set of translators doing their bit in Russian and Italian. The brewer would speak, in broad Derbyshire, then there would be a frantic muttering in the two foreign languages, with lots of 'Oohs' and 'Aahs' from the impressed guests, and finally I was left waiting for someone to translate Derbyshire dialect into standard English. The sampling made up for the wait though and, as I explained to Jane much later,

"I am sh-orry to keep you but you sh-ee, I am only an un-reconstipated (hic) - I mean un-reconstituted northerner!"

Jane now had to drive 'Auntie', which didn't please her. She has never really been fond of the old girl, nor have the rest of the family. Indeed, when my daughter was a teenager, she used to dive down on the back seat below window height if we passed anywhere near a group of her friends, so ashamed was she of being seen in such an old-fashioned car.

We retraced our way back down the bumpy lane to Hartington and on to our evening's rest, at a small caravan site nearby, just on the Derbyshire-Staffordshire border. We were staying in a mobile home but, by the looks of it, ours had not been mobile for many years. It was painted in what appeared to be camouflage colours, which worried me slightly because there was an army firing-range just down the road. Inside everything was like a doll's house, with tiny seats and tables, tiny sink and taps and a minute shower that would probably have suited hobbits better than us.

There wasn't space for both of us to move at the same time so we invented a sort of dance that involved skilful turning, bending and spinning, plus some conventions from the world of pantomime. However, it was clean and cheap (see 'Northern Stereotypes') and it had a most fantastic view down the Manifold Valley, over which the sun was now setting. We gazed at the sunset for a while and were gradually and gently changed from tense and frazzled human beings into jelly-like creatures, soft and emotional. It was so beautiful - as if the apricot clouds were the wake of some gorgeous galleon, departing our shores never to return, leaving behind marooned mankind.

At least it put me back in Jane's 'good books'.

Chapter 3
Thor's Cave and the Quiet Woman

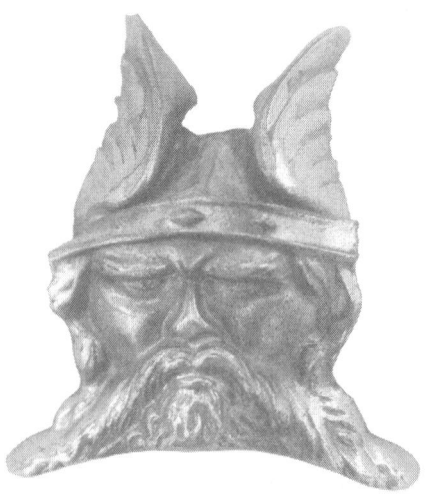

Auntie's bonnet badge

'To conquer a continent, to tame the shaggy roughness of
wild nature, means grim warfare'
- Theodore Roosevelt

Darkness, like a thick and suffocating blanket, was upon me. It smothered and imprisoned me. I was on my hands and knees with smooth, hard rock beneath me, crawling towards a slit of bright light that slashed, like a sharp knife, through the enfolding blackness. Gradually, an awareness of something incongruously domestic began to imprint itself onto my consciousness, a pastiche of the stifling cave that enclosed me and the interior of a caravan! What was a caravan doing in this black hole?

I opened my eyes and woke up. Someone was kneeling on top of me with their hands around my throat. It was Jane! I faced death for the second time in twenty-four hours.

"What are you doing?" I gasped, making a mental note to cancel my life assurance policy.

The love of my life stared down at me with unseeing, dead-mackerel eyes. Did I mention that my wife sleepwalks?

"I want to crumple you up," she pronounced in a strange, robotic monotone.

This sounded vaguely interesting but also potentially unpleasant. I needed more information.

"Move over," she muttered, "there's a tractor coming."

This definitely wasn't the comment of anybody conscious. Fortunately, I am used to these sorts of ramblings and night wanderings. They are rare and usually reflect a little anxiety; I suppose that after the previous day it was only to be expected. I managed to extricate myself and, coming back to reality, Jane yawned and smiled.

"I was having a lovely dream," she said.

As it was daylight we both got up sleepily and bumped around our mobile home. I was still alive, and it promised to be a good day. Some friends of ours were joining us for a walk in the hills. A good, brisk hike always invigorates the frame, doesn't it?

During breakfast memories of hiking expeditions drifted nostalgically through my mind. I had been a boy scout in my youth. Now *there's* a great English tradition. Remember those exciting camping trips to obscure parts of the country, only to find yourself sleeping in smelly tents, with people that you didn't really know, still less like? Remember dib-dib-dib and dob-dob-dob, and woggles? There was a great game we used to play called 'Split the Kipper', which involved throwing a sheath knife close to someone else's feet. Wherever the knife landed your opponent had to stretch one foot to that place. The aim was to try and get them to do the splits. Can you imagine the health and safety implications for such a game these days? And then there was the smell of dubbin on gigantic, overweight hiking boots. It was great preparation for life. I was ready for Thor's Cave.

Thor's Cave was our intended destination for the day. This dramatic sounding place must have been in my dreams from the previous night because it is in fact a cathedral-like cavern in the face of a limestone cliff. It stands high above the old, disused track of the Leek-Manifold Light Railway and it is a truly fitting dwelling for the God of Thunder. The trail is now beloved of cyclists and walkers and winds along the Manifold Valley, beside the river. There is an interesting tunnel you can whistle and hoot your way through to get an echo, and a little further along you come to Wetton Mill. Wetton Mill is a former flour mill but these days it is more popular for the café, picnics and messing about in the river.

A stone's throw from the mill the River Manifold suddenly dries up. One minute you have quite a wide, fast flowing body of water and the next it just disappears, without so much as a gurgle, leaving barely a trickle. It is as if the river bed becomes porous. What happens is that the river dives underground into a series of what are called 'swallow holes'. These are subterranean tunnels formed by erosion and they consist of a honeycomb of limestone that takes the river four and a half miles to Ilam Park, where it rises again in a dramatic 'boil hole'.

About half a mile past the mill you turn a corner and suddenly there is Thor's Cave - so called I suppose because it is on such an impressive scale. It would definitely provide a suitable home for the Norse god. You could imagine him flying out wielding his hammer, perhaps after a domestic with Mrs Thor, and smiting the mountain with shivering power. To climb up to this home of the god was our objective. Even from the foot of the cliff path the entrance to the cave yawned mightily at us and we girded our loins in anticipation. The Viking blood was stirring!

Next time you are sitting in your car at traffic lights and you are lucky enough to have an old Rover pull up behind you, look in your rear-view mirror. As your mouth drops open at the sight of a massive radiator grille filling your back window you may notice the chrome effigy of the head of a Viking, glaring at you sternly. To me this emblem of Rover cars resonates with a fierce determination and strength. What a great symbol for 'The Backbone of Britain'! I don't know if the modern Land Rover still uses this. They are now owned by the Indian company 'Tata' (Tay-ter?) so perhaps they use a Maris Piper as a bonnet badge.

I thought of my chrome Viking as I assessed the climb and then of the scout motto, 'Be prepared'! How fit are you? Don't pretend, be honest with yourself! As we all looked up, each of us keeping the realistic estimation of our fitness level to ourselves, we solemnly declared that this ascent would be no problem for us - a mere bagatelle. The path wound through the trees up the side of a steep gorge and we set off with an air of nonchalant bravado, trying to outdo each other with extravagant shows of energy and gusto.

The first intimation that this climb was going to be a little more demanding than anticipated was the gradual petering out of conversation. At first we talked animatedly about a range of subjects both temporal and spiritual. With furrowed brows and strong hand gestures we talked the government out of office and comprehensively put the world to rights.

After a little time however, I noticed that my companions' contributions were becoming somewhat truncated, accompanied by short grunts, exclamations and exhalations of breath. Indeed, my own points of view were now being conveyed it seemed using mostly facial expressions, and I tried to vary these to show agreement or disagreement. Nevertheless, we continued to climb at a ridiculous pace, and shortly we all began perspiring heavily and turning various shades of puce. You see, we knew that we were men, British men, and that to slacken the pace meant disgrace. Was it worth a heart attack or stroke? Apparently, for we all landed at the top together, lathered in sweat and giving each other very little eye contact, whilst we found something unique and distant to stare at for about five minutes.

There is, of course, quite a lot to stare at from the mouth of Thor's Cave. It is a good vantage point from which to observe the action of glacial erosion. When the ice caps retreated (yes, they have left the North) they created a high plateau in the White Peak, bisected by many river valleys. Because limestone is relatively soft you do get some dramatically shaped peaks but they are all of a similar height, which gives an idea of the original level of the plateau.

You can see lots of green copper roofs from this elevation which is evidence of the fact that it used to be mined round here. Actually, copper from these hills can be found on the roof tops of famous buildings all over the world, such as the cathedrals of Florence and Chartres. The 4th Duke of Devonshire owned the mines in the 18th century and he made a profit of £300,000 from them (a huge amount for the time) and that he used the money to build The Crescent in Buxton. It has been said that the copper from round here was used to 'copper-bottom the fleet and to roof the world'.

Thor's Cave is one of many sprinkled throughout the White Peak and sometimes these caves develop into whole systems of underground caverns, centred around Castleton. There you can find Speedwell Cavern and Treak Cliff Cavern, and (the prettily named) 'Devil's Arse' Cavern.

Up close Thor's Cave looms over you - a massive, gaping hole in the side of a crag. It invites exploration and a quick scramble up a slippery slope takes you into the mouth of the cave proper. When your eyes have adjusted to the darkness a soaring arched roof is revealed, very like the structure of a gothic cathedral. It is big enough for the home of a god but seems more suited to be the lair of some enormous dragon, standing guard over a treasure of local copper. So atmospheric is the location that it has been used in films, such as 'The Lair of the White Worm', a 1988 horror film by Ken Russell, and starring a young Hugh Grant. Archaeological digs have found evidence of human habitation dating back over 10,000 years; they found pottery, stone tools, jewellery and the bones of extinct animals. I think they might have been victims of the White Worm!

Disappointingly, the cave comes to an abrupt end fairly quickly and the only other bit to explore is a much smaller opening at one side, through which light streams narrowly from outside. It seemed possible, just, to squeeze through this small exit, and I will now tell a cautionary tale about the importance of behaving sensibly in such situations. One of our party (not me I hasten to add) suggested that we all exit by this tiny hole and descend to the valley floor, freestyle as it were. Wouldn't that be a fun, exciting and manly thing to do? Nobody wanted to seem like a wet lettuce and so no one demurred in any way from this barmy proposition. We all pretended to look casual and unconcerned and agreement was given in little nods and affirmative monosyllables. If I tell you that this crag is a favourite haunt of the British Mountaineering Club, which rates climbs here as ranging from 'Very Severe' to 'Extreme 7', then it will help you to appreciate the stupidity of this idea.

When I say that nobody dismissed this plan, I mean the men. Of course, our right-minded wives had agreed to return by the recommended route, and turned rather baleful eyes on us as we left for our appointment with fate.

Initially, the decision appeared to be quite a good one. Each of us manoeuvred through the hole and immediately outside there seemed to be a path heading down towards the tree-line, albeit a very steep one. We headed off downwards, with an exaggeratedly relaxed attitude, no one wanting to show that inwardly he was a gibbering wreck. It was a dirt path with limestone chippings mixed in and with roots from sundry vegetation acting as a border. It had probably been made by sheep or goats, certainly something more sure-footed than a group of mere blokes. We began to slip and slide as it dived and angled more acutely, and the roots became handgrips to stop us plummeting headlong. The self-appointed leader raised his voice to make encouraging noises as his fast disintegrating macho party began flailing around wildly, scrambling for any purchase they could on the lethally precipitous ground.

Things might have turned nasty if the trees hadn't arrived when they did. Already people had turned over onto their stomachs and were edging down backwards, treading on each other's fingers and grimacing with effort and pain. Thankfully, the trees provided hand-holds and foot-rests so we were able to swing our way to the valley floor like a troupe of gibbons. Now we had reached relative safety it was only a matter of time before we descended to face the music. Far below I could make out our sensible wives, who had reached the bottom long ago, gazing at us with a mixture of incredulity and horror.

"We were ten minutes away from calling out Mountain Rescue," said Jane on the way back. "What is it with men?"

I couldn't really answer that. They say that the male psyche is much simpler than the female but I am not so sure; it is certainly different. Men like showing off their physical prowess but, as we had just proved, this can lead to stupidly dangerous situations. Men are happy pottering about in a shed, fiddling with bits of wood or wiring, or sticking their nose under the bonnet of an old car like 'Auntie'. My male friends are keen on sharing the inner workings of a carburettor but their wives just want to use 'Auntie' for weddings. I am quite content with this arrangement because I like a wide audience to appreciate her charms and it gives me a chance to buff up the old girl and decorate her with ribbons. The rear opening back doors (known as 'suicide doors') with internal running boards are perfect for a bride and her train to alight. Once, when I was getting 'Auntie' ready for a friend's wedding in Norfolk, I was just greasing the hinges of the rear door to try and stop an annoying squeak when the postman walked past.

"Got a groan on it?" he asked in a broad Norfolk accent, without pausing in the delivery of the post. I love this use of idiomatic English. When 'Auntie' had been polished to perfection a Lancashire guest paused to comment

"Doesn't she look bonny?"

It felt like the events of the day had lasted a lifetime and when I thought about Thor's Cave I became weak and jittery. It was time to do something more convivial and less dangerous so we all decided to call in at the local country fair. I tend to get bored at country fairs where the raciest stuff on offer is usually attractions such as 'Guess the Weight of the Cake', or 'Take a Ride on a Tractor', but today it was just what I needed.

The fair at Hartington appeared at first to be fairly typical. There was an abundance of home made jam and chutney for sale, and a large variety of cheeses, including some from the local Stilton producer. Derbyshire is one of only three counties allowed to call their cheese Stilton, the other two being Leicestershire and Nottinghamshire, but recently the county of Cambridgeshire has been making a claim for fame as the inventor of the cheese. This is not an unreasonable claim you might think because the actual village of Stilton lies in Cambridgeshire. The plot thickens however (or curdles) by the assertions of the citizens of Melton Mowbray in Leicestershire that *they* were the first to produce Stilton cheese, and that it only became known as Stilton because of an insatiable craving for the stuff on the part of the inhabitants of Stilton village. The story goes that in the 18th century the cheese had to be imported (from Melton Mowbray) into Stilton, in such large quantities that it eventually became synonymous with the village.

From the conflicting evidence it looks as if the 'cheese wars' might get dirty and I wouldn't want to be on the receiving end of a 17lb Stilton so I think I will leave the subject there. There was something far more fascinating at the fair than cheese as far as I was concerned and I was drawn to it by the existence of a small crowd gathered round a paddock. In the centre of the paddock was a cow, which seemed to be the object of peoples' attention. The cow wasn't doing anything out of the ordinary as far as I could tell. It mooched about unhurriedly, munching the grass and occasionally looking at the rapt onlookers and mooing. However, the crowd found this absorbing and noted carefully every little move the cow made. I wondered what on earth they could possibly find so interesting in this particular bovine when there were thousands of such animals doing the very same things in the surrounding countryside. Then I noticed that the paddock had been divided into squares, each of about two yards in length, using whitewash to mark the grass; not only that but there appeared to be some fairly intense activity going on in a booth at one corner.

Leaving scrutiny of the cow I wandered over to the booth and found a jolly, red-faced man addressing an audience of twenty or so people. He was pointing at a blackboard and easel on which it was possible to discern crudely chalked squares, which I took to represent the paddock, and people had put their signatures on some of them.

His voice suddenly rose to a cry,

"Roll up, roll up! Guess which square the cow is going to muck in, and win £20! Don't be shy ladies and gentlemen; she's well primed and ready to fire. Win £10 in the event of a tie."

I was entranced; that's why the crowd was watching the poor beast so intently – to see where it would crap!

Good money was changing hands and I was tempted to have a bet, but I thought that maybe it would be some time before the subject 'performed', and our friends had to return home soon. I couldn't help speculating whether this 'sport', like many others where money changes hands, was prone to cheating in some way. Perhaps they 'fixed' the cow so that it became constipated. On the other hand, perhaps they tried to give it diarrhoea - in order to spread the betting. The possibilities for puns were endless.

It was time for an evening meal in a more fragrant atmosphere so we said goodbye to our friends and returned to our caravan to change and shower. I had been thoroughly chastened by the descent from the cave but the cow pat competition had done much to restore my normally cheerful disposition as we set off in 'Auntie' to look for a local hostelry.

Many years of exhaustive research have put me in the happy position of knowing the pubs in this area pretty well. One quaintly titled establishment, not far from Thor's Cave, is 'The Quiet Woman' at Earl Sterndale, which has on its sign a picture of a woman without a head! There are many quiet not to say remote pubs in the Pennines and we decided to experiment with a place in one of the more inaccessible valleys. After getting lost several times we finally pulled up to the car park of our chosen venue, sending a group of scratching hens diving for cover. It was going dark, which did not help our first impression of the place. It was a very old and somewhat dilapidated building, with vines covering the entire frontage and partially obscuring the small windows. There was a rabbit cage blocking the doorway and only an old sign, dangling precariously from a tree, gave any indication that this was indeed a public house. Nevertheless, a dim light struggled through one of the windows and, because I am not easily put off entering a pub, we decided to screw our courage to the sticking place and go in.

As we got out of the car a mist was beginning to descend, curling around the neighbouring buildings, rendering everything mysterious. And wasn't that a dog howling somewhere in the distance? We quickly scuttled inside, squeezing past the rabbit, and entered the lounge bar - in fact the only bar. You know those black and white films where a fashionable couple from London, on holiday in Devon, get lost and break down in a storm on Dartmoor? They enter the local pub seeking help and immediately it goes quiet and people stop what they are doing to stare at these rain-soaked sophisticates. Well, that is more or less what happened here, except we weren't rain-soaked or sophisticated. In this instance the locals happened to be a group of women huddled round a fire, all of them wearing dressing-gowns and slippers. They stared at us though, long and hard. They could not have looked more surprised if we had been aliens, or stark naked.

I suppose it was the women round the fire who first made me think of the witches in Macbeth. What if we had caught them just before they were to perform one of their abominable rites? That would explain the dressing gowns; underneath they were obviously completely 'starkers' and any moment now they were going to jump up and dance in front of the fire, invoking diabolical agents to bring them a human sacrifice. Clearly we had been drawn there for such a purpose! Quickly I looked round for means of a swift exit, or at least for a goat that might do as a substitute.

I was brought back to my senses by my wife greeting the women and unconcernedly asking if we might order a drink. The spell was broken and one of the ladies got up and crossed over to the bar. She smiled and apologised for her attire but they didn't often get visitors in the evening at this time of year. She poured our drinks and looked sympathetically at my wife.

"Is your husband alright?" she enquired, managing to inject all sorts of nuances into the word 'alright'. I took offence at this remark and tried to replace my worried expression with a nonchalant one.

"Perfectly well, thank you," I remarked, with as much sophistication as I could muster, and ushered my better half to a table.

The rest of the evening passed uneventfully for the quiet woman and me. For supper we enjoyed a delicious old-fashioned stew, with dumplings.

I still wonder though whether those women were in league with the devil.

Chapter 4
The Two Seater

*'Something old, something new,
something borrowed, something blue'*

It was time to get out the costumes. We had planned our trip to coincide with two weddings en route, and the first one promised to be 'different'. It was to take place outdoors, in a wood on top of The Roaches - a rocky outcrop between Hartington and Leek. Not only that, the whole performance was to be in the style of the ancient Celtic tradition – hence the costumes! The wedding invitation had contained detailed drawings of how Celts dressed and we faithfully tried to reproduce these. Jane spent hours working away at a sewing machine and finally managed an approximation of Celtic garb. We changed into our costumes, somewhat furtively, in our rented mobile home and stood in front of a mirror to examine the results. Jane didn't look too bad. She was wearing an off-the-shoulder number made from one long piece of material, in a sort of bog green colour. She would look good in anything, whereas I on the other hand looked like a reject from The Flintstones. My peat brown, toga-type outfit was too short and worse, it kept slipping off me completely so that I was in mortal danger of flashing the bride and groom.

The plan was to visit Leek market in the morning and then drive to The Roaches after lunch for the wedding.

"But," I protested, "I can't wander round Leek dressed like this - I'll get arrested."

"We'll change in the toilets of a pub," said Jane. "You'll be fine."

I was dubious but agreed to this arrangement and so we set off for Leek. The drive from Hartington to Leek took us up and over the Staffordshire Moorlands, through Reapsmoor. These moorlands rise to 1,500ft and represent the only bit of Staffordshire to stray into the Pennine Chain. There is an army firing range on Reapsmoor, which also used to function as an exciting playground for my nephews when they were young. They would turn up, their pockets stuffed full of ordnance, and cheerfully fill up the kitchen table with bullets and bits of shell casing. I am sure that we were only inches away from being blown up but they were happy days!

Leek is known hereabouts as the 'Queen of the Moorlands' because it is such a sweet and graceful place. It has a market, which is held on Wednesdays and Saturdays. There is the indoor market, which goes back to Victorian times, and an outdoor market in the town square. The indoor market sells mainly food but also the inevitable stock in trade of the English market - slippers, tea towels etc., plus a veritable array of man-made fibre-based products. The outdoor market sells mostly 'fruit and veg' but on Saturdays it has a brilliant 'flea-market'.

I wondered if I might find an interesting pipe at the market to add to my collection, or maybe a pipe rack to hold them in. The most unwieldy thing I ever bought there was a set of bookshelves. It was at a time when our daughter was a babe-in-arms and we happened to be in my other car, an MGB GT two seater sports car. My teal-blue MG was a great little hatchback and was ideal (I convinced Jane) for carrying prams and baby paraphernalia. It was not strictly a two seater because it had a tiny bench-like back seat. I had had a seat-belt fitted to this, which I reckoned would last until our girl was about six years old, after which time her head would probably hit the roof.

One particular Saturday I got very excited because I found a bargain. We had needed another bookshelf for some time, to house my ever increasing library, and this particular set of shelves was an ideal size – ideal for holding books that is, not necessarily for transporting in a sports car. The trouble was that the shelves were six feet high by three feet wide, but I reckoned they would fit. We bought the offending item and transported it turtle-fashion to the car. Jane was not at all sure this was going to work but I assured her that I could *make* it work. I did make it work. The car boot was just over three feet wide and with some sweating and cursing we managed to wedge the set of shelves in. However, being six feet in length it now stretched right over the rear seat leaving only room for one stooping passenger in the front. What was worse it still stuck out at the back by a considerable distance, in a decidedly illegal way, and what were we going to do with the baby?

My solution was to have Jane sitting low in the front seat with Katherine in her arms and the top of the bookshelves on the back of her neck. The boot lid was left open and tied with cord, which then went round the protruding shelves. This was madness I know, but who can put old heads on young shoulders? I should just be grateful that we got home with any heads at all. To avoid attention I drove back by the steepest most circuitous lanes through the Staffordshire Moorlands, via the Roaches and the Goyt Valley.

Today the market was in full swing as we arrived. Something to look out for here (as well as pipes) is ceramics, in other words, pots. Leek is a town full of pots and potters. This is because it lies on the eastern edge of the Potteries, the five towns which form the centre of the ceramics industry in Britain.

Disappointingly, not so many pots are made there now as in days gone by, but you can still find big names like Wedgwood and Spode and visit their factory shops. At these you might pick up an exquisite soup tureen, a dinner service or a variety of china figurines at bargain prices. Please be careful though wandering around the showroom because, with one sweep of an unguarded coat, you could find yourself looking at a bill for £700, for a Spode soup tureen!

Leek is my favourite town in the southern Pennines because it is not pretentious in any way, despite its informal title of 'queen'. It does have attractive buildings of historical note, and interesting shops and pubs, but it 'holds them lightly'; it doesn't give itself 'airs'. Leek is a Norman name and the town came to the fore as a centre for the dyeing and textile industries. It specialised in the manufacture of silk, although, sadly, the last remaining worm passed on in 1994!

In the 19th century William Morris studied here to learn about dyes and dyeing, which became an essential feature of his Arts and Crafts movement. He wrote about the town in a series of essays called 'Bijou Leek', and he helped design some new buildings in the Arts and Crafts style. Many local churches still have embroidery that dates back to Morris' time.

Despite this rich vein of history Leek doesn't push its pedigree in your face. What it does push in your face is the Staffordshire Oatcake; they are all over the place in the town and they are delicious. Staffordshire

Oatcakes are not like the Scottish variety; they are a combination of oatmeal, flour and yeast, cooked on a griddle. They look like a type of pancake, about nine inches in diameter, and at one time they formed the staple diet of hungry potters. Many houses used to sell oatcakes directly from their front window but these days it is usually shops that sell them as a takeaway dish. I know of one place in Leek that looks just like a fish and chip shop, but it sells only oatcakes, with a vast choice of different fillings. My favourite is cheese and bacon which, I am sure, is terribly unhealthy. Whilst Jane was looking at shoes I sneaked off to this tiny takeaway and got myself one!

The forerunner of the oatcake was a strangely named dish called 'Lumptytums'. This was a bit like porridge but somehow managed to preserve a lump of warm, doughy oatmeal in the centre. It was reputedly very sustaining and a testimony to the bonny lasses of the Pennines, as remembered in the old rhyme:

'Lumptytums, Lumptytums, Lumptytums,
The rosiest cheeks and the plumpest bums,
Are the girls who are fed on Lumptytums'

As Jane finished her purchases I thought about the 'Lumptytums' rhyme and wondered what evidence existed for its central assertion.

Another reason I like Leek is the people – they are so friendly. Everyone will chat to you - in the shops, the banks, and on the market. They call you 'duck' round here, in the same vein that they call you 'love' further north. Even the men call you 'duck' (or maybe it is just me). A friendly atmosphere pervades the town in a way that I don't find common nowadays. Why is this I wonder? Is our respect and regard for one another leaching away in this country? We charge about, seemingly oblivious to the existence of others anymore. I seem to remember a time when people were more courteous and obliging. Take a wander around Leek market and get chatting to someone, that's my advice.

We had now completed our wandering around and decided to find a pub for lunch (I am afraid that I didn't own up to having already eaten!) The choice of a pub is always difficult, especially in Leek. You have 'The Roebuck', which is a very friendly place, or 'The Wilkes Head', which serves the best beer, plus lots of others. We settled for 'The Abbey Inn', which is on the road north of the town, close to Rudyard Lake and Tittesworth Water. The writer Rudyard Kipling was named after Rudyard Lake because it was the place his parents first met, in 1863. Thank goodness they didn't meet at Tittesworth Water.

The Abbey Inn is built on the site of an ancient abbey (now sadly gone), called Dieulacres. Like most abbeys it was destroyed during the Reformation and you can see that many of the old stones were used to build the pub. There are several pretty walks to be had round here and we let Meg have a romp about, because we didn't know if dogs were allowed in the pub. She really resented going back in the car and looked reproachfully at us.

I was somewhat nervous throughout lunch, even though it consisted of Staffordshire Oatcakes, because I knew that I would soon have to change into an Ancient Celt. I would go into the toilet as mere Pete Lancaster and emerge moments later as Super Druid! As it happened I needn't have worried. When I emerged shyly from the loo the Landlord took one look at me and announced loudly,

"Ah, another one for the wedding!" and everybody cheered. Jane, of course, got wolf-whistled.

However, things never seem to work out straightforwardly for me. Doom and disaster stalk me at all times. As 'Auntie' descended a long hill on the way to the wedding I applied the brakes…and nothing happened; fresh air! Brake failure had never happened to me before and it is an experience I would not want to repeat. To put your foot on the brake pedal and for it to suddenly give way and plop to the floor makes for a heart-stopping moment. There is a sensation of shock first, swiftly followed by a flood of panic, which washes in as the car begins to accelerate downwards.

I tried to pull into the car park of 'The Rock Tavern' but we were going too fast. I knew what the problem was with the brakes - they had got air in the system - but I never imagined that it would cause a problem like this. It is strange what your brain does in such situations. It started to work very quickly, which is unusual for me, not just on the trouble in hand but on a whole range of other issues as well.

Bizarrely, the bit of doggerel about 'Lumptytums' kept running through my head as we spiralled down the hill, increasingly out of control. I wrestled with the gear stick on 'Auntie' to jam it into a lower gear and managed to get to second, but there was no synchromesh for first and so we continued to plummet. I risked a swift look at Jane but she was nowhere to be seen; then I noticed her huddled figure in the foot well of the passenger side, curled up foetus-like.

"Sorry," I said, "there's a small leak on the brake-fluid tubing."

I am afraid it would be somewhat inappropriate to record the reply from the foot well.

We were now travelling at a great rate of knots and I was grateful that there was no other traffic around. 'Whose fault was it that the brakes had failed?' I thought. 'Was it my garage? Was it those wretched engineers at the Rover works at Longbridge? Was I going to be able to keep down my lunchtime oatcake? Perhaps the fact that the car was forty-odd years old meant that parts were bound to start failing. Ah, that might be it. What satisfaction there was to be had in the knowledge of precisely why we were going to die!

Next I tried to stop the car with the handbrake, but it had little effect. I started to wonder if it would hurt when we crashed. I hope that I am not too afraid of death but I am not keen on the idea of dying, particularly at a relatively young age. There were so many things still to do and opportunities to learn, or even for me to become a better person; then I might be better prepared. Also, I couldn't bear the thought of being responsible for injuring or killing Jane.

I desperately ranged about for a lay-by, a side road, or even a large pile of sand! Meg barked excitedly and licked my face (dogs have no sense of occasion).

All might have gone badly but for those very engineers at Longbridge who had designed this vehicle in the post war years. I started to pump the brakes up and down vigorously and after a few, seemingly endless, moments some bite began to return to them. The air was pushed out and brake fluid trickled back in to power the servo. With 'backward mutterings of dissevering power' the leaping car began to slow and then, blessedly, to stop by the side of the road.

We were pale and shaking, but alive and unhurt. Jane climbed out of the foot well and regarded me ominously. I guess the things she said to me were justified but I found them a little hurtful and I certainly wasn't going to push 'Auntie' off the nearest cliff, as she was suggesting, and then jump after her.

After a few moments we headed gingerly for a nearby garage. The mechanic there was both sympathetic and helpful. It transpired that 'Auntie' just required a piece of rubber tubing, because brake fluid had been seeping out of the perished original. 'It would only take him a few minutes' he said. 'Did we know 'The Yew Tree' pub down the road'? Actually we did. This pub has featured in national newspapers over the years because it is quite simply unique. It used to be run by two old ladies who would dress up each night in high-collared ruched blouses and their hair in tight buns, not because they were trying to wear costume but because they actually grew up in the Edwardian era!

The pub has a collection of Polyphons, those enormous precursors of the record player, plus other sundry antiques, including a 'patent dog-carrier', hanging above the bar. This consisted of a metal frame in the shape of a whippet. Apparently the dog puts its head in the metal muzzle and then its body is encased in metal strapping. At the rear end is a hinged flap with a screw to turn on it, in order to secure the dog. You can guess where the screw socket is! I hoped it was only a joke item.

Jane and I waited rather forlornly in the bar, a sad pair of Ancient Celts, whilst the garage man worked on 'Auntie'. I walked over to the lounge window to see what progress he was making when I was halted by a surprising discovery. Standing proudly amongst the dusty settles and illuminated dimly by the ancient electricity system was the finest two seater I have ever seen. It gleamed dully under many layers of brown varnish, a masterpiece of efficient design and function. Was it a Ferrari you ask, or a Maserati? Maybe it was an Aston Martin. Well, you would be wrong. It was, in fact, a magnificent two seater toilet! To be technically correct it was just the toilet seats and, I hastily add, now used purely for decorative purposes. I was awe-struck. What a concept – twin seats! In what dark furnace of an architect's imagination did this contraption take shape? Imagine chatting with your neighbour as you both reach for a sheet of Bronco, or exchanging pleasantries with them after a good curry. It must be very convivial.

Of course, many terraced houses had this arrangement in the 19th and 20th centuries. Before main drains were installed they used to collect the effluence with a giant ladle and take it away by lorry, a system that prevails to this day in some of the remoter Pennine villages. I vividly remember being enchanted with my grandmother's outside loo, in Brighouse in the 1950s. My father told me that when he was a boy he used to wait until the old lady next door was ensconced and then he would take a previously prepared small paper boat, set fire to it and then float it along the open drain until it disappeared under the wall of the engaged privy. He was a rascal!

Soon the car was ready and it was high time to get to the wedding. If you travel out of Leek on the road to Buxton you will notice an unusual rocky outcrop called The Roaches, which has been shaped into some interesting formations by the moorland winds. They look like bad examples of modern sculpture or the set from a film about Easter Island. They are also responsible for the name of a local pub, 'The Winking Man'. At one point as you drive past there is a rock formation in the shape of a silhouette of a man's face. When you reach a fixed point the 'man' winks at you. Of course, it is the light flashing through a chink in the rock and it is gone in a moment, but the effect is startling. Unsurprisingly, the pub's name is unique, although there is a 'Winking Frog' and a 'Blinking Owl'.

On top of the Roaches was the place chosen for the ceremony by the earnest young advocates of Celtic Christianity, whose wedding we had nearly missed. I wasn't really looking forward to standing around for ages, freezing to death in a wood, dressed like a twit. Much to my surprise some guests had obviously misunderstood, or not really bothered to follow, the detailed instructions on their invitations for how to dress as an Ancient Celt; or maybe they were simply unable to sew. Whatever the reason it became apparent that many had simply dropped in to their nearest fancy-dress shop and picked up whatever was available at the time. Consequently, we had everything from Widow Twankey to Charles I in the congregation. The only reason I managed to find the venue as quickly as I did was by following a succession of historical or pantomime characters across the Staffordshire countryside. I knew we were on the right track when I noticed a monk having a quick drag (I mean a cigarette) under a bridge by the side of the road.

The minister taking the ceremony had gamely dressed up as Friar Tuck or something and he presided benevolently over the service. The plan was for the bride-to-be to make her entrance through a glade in the wood, carried on a litter by four groomsmen. They turned out to consist of two Celtic priests, a Jedi

Knight and Puss-in-Boots. I could have stopped myself from getting a fit of the giggles even then but unfortunately the bride, who was wearing a tall conical hat of the type beloved by a damsel in distress, kept getting her veil caught on overhanging branches. This resulted in the litter being pulled this way and that and it was all the bearers could do to keep the poor girl from pitching onto the forest floor.

I suppose all's well that ends well – Friar Tuck gave a sincere and touching address and Charles I kept wiping the tears away on his ruff. Later we all sat on straw bales and played authentic Celtic games but what really made the day for me was the whole roast hog turning gently on a spit. I started to feel like a proper Viking (I mean Celt!).

Chapter 5
The Wisdom of Solomon

For the third day in a row I had come face to face with death. What a great holiday this was turning out to be. I felt bad about the car but Jane forgave me - yet again.

"After all," she said, smiling, "we have a common allergy."

A 'common allergy'…? It is enough to know that my dear wife often misplaces words, both extravagantly and ingeniously, much to my puzzlement, and often delight. Once, while talking over the fence to a neighbour who was shelling peas in the garden, she asked, quite innocently,

"Are you pea-ing in the garden?"

The man looked at her suspiciously and didn't reply. Jane had a vague sense that she had offended him but didn't know how, so she followed it up with a blinder of a supplementary:

"It's nice pea-ing in the garden, isn't it?"

For 'common allergy' she meant 'commonality'. I couldn't argue with that.

Seeking a quiet day we decided to meander towards Buxton, via Carsington Water. This is not a direct route but it did at least sound safe as it is fairly level, until you approach Buxton.

Carsington is a pleasant body of water to the southeast of Hartington. It was built as a reservoir during the 1980s and opened formally in 1992, by the Queen. It was formed by damming the River Derwent and flooding the valley below the villages of Brassington and Kirk Ireton. We had planned on going for a walk but unfortunately, my Ordnance Survey map was so old that it didn't feature the reservoir and so it kept trying to take us on footpaths that would have led to a watery grave. Eventually we circumnavigated the nine mile reservoir and ended up where we wanted to be, at 'The Barley Mow Inn' at Kirk Ireton. 'The Barley Mow' proved to be an ancient pub with an old range in the bar area and beer served from the barrel. After I had had a pint I went to the hatch to ask for another. The old lady behind the bar stared hard at me.

"No!" she retorted to my request. "You can't have another drink."

I was a trifle flummoxed by this response and was about to reassure the woman that I wasn't driving when she cut in,

"A real drinker always brings his pots back."

Ah, so that was the problem – I had left my pint pot on the table. She didn't want to have to use another glass. This amused the bloke standing next to me. He told me not to worry and that this was quite the norm here. After our little misunderstanding had been cleared up I got chatting to the guy. He told me that he had worked on the construction of Carsington Water, many years ago. What, I wondered, had been his job?

"I was a stick-boy" he said.

Apparently, he used to collect the dead wood off the floor of the valley before it was flooded and then burn it. This was to stop it becoming flotsam and jetsam, floating on the surface of the water.

After lunch we headed back to Carsington and by the time we reached the car park where 'Auntie' was waiting we were thirsty, so we decided to grab a cup of tea at the visitor centre. The visitor centre has quite a lot of things to look at, buy or experience and Severn-Trent Water have done a good job in developing the site. As well as shops and a café there is a sailing club, an adventure playground, nature trails and cycle- hire facilities. In the main atrium you can find a whole host of water-based exhibits and hands-on attractions. The best of these is a giant, circular stone-ball, kept permanently supported by a jet of water about half an inch above its base. The ball weighs one ton but you can turn it with just one finger, buoyed up as it is by water power. I found this quite remarkable, as did a small boy of about eight, who happened to be visiting with his family at the same time as us. He proved to be a real pain. He was loud and obnoxious and looking for trouble. He kept trying to push the ball off its watery base, much to the consternation and embarrassment of his parents. They remonstrated with the boy ineffectually but soon gave up, leaving him to engage, Sysiphus-like, in some major boulder rolling.

It was time to bring in the matriarch...cue Grandma! The parents sat down passively to watch as this aged warrior girded her bum bag and prepared for combat. Her approach was subtle - at first she talked gently to her prey, smiling and appealing to him. But all the time she was moving closer, until she was in striking distance. The wayward child had stopped trying to dislodge the ball by now, as he gradually fell under Grandma's spell. Eventually, he just stood, looking somewhat stupefied, with his hands by his sides and his mouth open, awaiting his fate. The coup-de-grace came soon enough. Grandma's soft words and concerned expression suddenly changed and like a hissing cobra she struck out and sent the boy sprawling. The parents seemed pleased and led out their now bawling offspring. Grandma coolly regarded the small crowd of onlookers and, hitching up her bum bag again, turned on her heel and swaggered after the rest of the family. I suppose she was wrong to hit the boy but it did seem to demonstrate the operation of poetic justice.

Crossing the ford at Tissington, we carried on towards Buxton but we had one more port of call before our sojourn. Just off the road between Leek and Buxton, below Axe Edge, you see a sign for Flash, officially the highest village in the whole of Britain. This title was conferred by the Guinness Book of Records and later reinforced by the BBC and the Ordnance Survey in 2007, after a challenge from Wanlockhead in Dumfries and Galloway. The name 'Flash' may refer to a sudden moving body of water, as in 'flash flood'. In Cheshire they call a lake a 'flash,' usually ones that appear quickly, in abandoned sand quarries.

In the 18th century the villagers of Flash used to make buttons for the nearby silk trade in Leek. For this they used button-presses, and all went well until a group of local rogues and vagabonds realised that the same button-presses could be used for minting counterfeit coins of the realm. The coins were exchanged at the nearby pub 'The Three Shires' but the scam was eventually discovered and the perpetrators hanged. It is said that we get the expression 'flash money' from this little enterprise, meaning money that is not 'secure' or based on something dishonest.

There are most of the things necessary for life in Flash – a pub, a chapel, a school (and no shops!). The chapel stands opposite the pub, as is often the case in villages. I do think it is a shame that the two establishments have become mutually exclusive in the eyes of some peoples. A bit further along is a farm that belongs to a charity, where disadvantaged young people are helped back into society; a sort of 'halfway house'. The charity looks after these teenagers and tries to give them skills for possible employment in the future. It also gives them life skills and thereby some belief in themselves. This was the reason for our detour to Flash. We had called in to see a young friend of ours who we had got to know through his foster parent. Johnny (not his real name) had had a troubled upbringing in quite a rough area of Manchester. He seemed pleased to see us and was keen to demonstrate that he could now drive a tractor. We spent some time with him looking at his room and listening whilst he went through his daily routine here, along with the other boys. I reflected later on what a lot of good this establishment was doing, probably unsung and largely ignored by the world around.

Johnny did make progress here but some time later he sadly ended up in the psychiatric unit of Hope Hospital in Salford. We visited him there and found it to be a depressing experience, not just because of the physical environment but because Johnny eventually withdrew into himself and refused to see us. If ever a place has a misnomer it is Hope.

On the other side of the coin (sorry) the village was also an early centre for Methodism, having a Methodist Chapel since 1784. The Methodists made a big impact in these hills and their legacy stands to this day in chapels up and down the Pennines. My father-in-law, Les, had been brought up in the Methodist tradition but he had stopped going to church in his youth for various reasons. In his last years he developed dementia sadly, but before he died he attended a few services at the church Jane and I attend, which is not of the Methodist persuasion. When it comes to worship I am of a conservative nature, fearful of making an exhibition of myself. I suppose I am what Yorkshire folk might call 'stuck-up like a piece of burnt leather'. I just stand there and mumble the responses. Jane is much more lively however and never happier than when she is swaying to a song or hymn. She must have got it from Les because soon the both of them were bopping away like two of the Three Degrees. His enthusiasm didn't stretch to the sermons though and he would frequently turn round and say things like "It's boring this," in quite a loud voice.

Leaving Flash we carried on driving towards Buxton. From this direction the first hint of the town is Solomon's Temple, a 19th century folly which stands on a ridge high above the Georgian terraces and elegant parks below. I thought how it might be really useful to have Solomon's wisdom in order to sort out problem boys like Johnny.

Chapter 6
The Dukes of Hazard

> *Landowner: 'It takes me two days to*
> *drive across my property'.*
> *Me: 'Yes, I have a car like that too'.*

Our Pennine saga inevitably now brings us into the orbit of the Cavendish family, the Dukes of Devonshire, whose estate is centred on Chatsworth House, not far from Chesterfield. Already, in Hartington, you feel as if you are under the influence of one of the great families of the realm. The title of Marquis of Hartington is one that has belonged to the Devonshires for generations and you can see their crest carved onto the gables of many buildings both here and in the surrounding villages. By the time you reach Buxton the signs of their presence are everywhere.

Buxton is a gracious spa town with many notable buildings and beautiful parks. At the centre stands the Edwardian Opera House, with the Pavilion Gardens attached to it. Jane and I parked up here and wandered through the hot house, which has enormous African palms and Himalayan fronds. I love the warm and humid microclimate that pervades in such places. You could leave me here for hours, dodging amongst the shrubbery, and often Jane does so whilst she goes shopping, always remembering to collect me before I turn 'native'.

The Pavilion Gardens lead into a series of rooms of ever increasing size and faded grandeur, which host everything from tea dances to improvisational theatre. Today there was a Farmers' Market so I shuffled round the stalls looking for craft beers and homemade food. This is a great way to get a meal. You walk up to a stallholder, wearing your humble yet gullible expression (that takes time to master), and gaze uncertainly at their produce. Make as if to get something and then draw back. Invariably the brewer or farmer will step forward and encourage you to sample their wares. Repeat this process up and down the market until you are full, or until your wife comes to drag you away in disgust. Actually, I am not so mercenary; I normally buy something from a selection of the stalls, if not all.

I bought a bottle of beer with the alarming name of 'Kill your Darlings', and then, full of salami, cheese and country wine, I wandered out into the park and made my way to 'The Old Hall Hotel', which is held by some to be the oldest hotel in England. It stands opposite The Opera House and Pavilion Gardens, and has been here in one form or another since Roman times or earlier. The current building was built in 1573 by the Cavendish family and almost immediately became a fashionable meeting place. Mary Queen of Scots was kept under house arrest here from time to time between 1576 and1578. Her distinguished visitors included Lord Burghley and the Earls of Pembroke and Leicester. Mary was said to have enjoyed her summers here, sampling the waters and generally gadding about town, although she had to be back by 9pm before her curfew came into effect. When she left Mary etched a couplet on a bedroom window with a diamond ring, which can still be seen to this day. It reads:

'Buxton, whose warm waters have made thy name
    famous,
Perchance I shall visit thee no more – Farewell'.

Not particularly scintillating verse, but interesting nevertheless - if it is genuine!

The very oldest part of the hotel is the tower, which now houses the 'Paupers Pit Theatre', down in the very bowels of the building. This is the tiniest theatre you are ever likely to see. Jane hadn't arrived yet so I collected the key from the reception desk and descended a long flight of stairs to the ancient locked entrance at the bottom. I went into the black hole of the auditorium quietly and, as my eyes grew accustomed to the darkness, the sweetest little theatre appeared, with a tiny proscenium arch stage and a few rows of raked seats, ensuring an audience of no more than about thirty in total.

The theatre is used by a resident amateur dramatic group and also by touring theatre troupes (of modest size) as well as being pressed into service as a venue for Buxton's various arts festivals throughout the year. The only thing I found vaguely 'spooky' about it was its name. Perhaps it had been built on top of some ancient communal burial site for the poor – hence the name Paupers Pit. If you are on your own there then don't hang about!

Something tapped me on the shoulder and I nearly jumped out of my skin, but it was only Jane, who had returned from her shopping trip. We walked back up to reception and then into the restaurant for lunch. The restaurant of the hotel has a wonderful air of past glories and still does 'silver service', presided over by waitresses in crisp black dresses, white pinnies and bonnets. Previously, I had brought an aunt of mine here (not the Rover). She certainly knew how to behave in such establishments and, when she discovered a crumb on her fork, merely tapped the table with it loudly until a waitress came running; she then handed it to her without a word.

There is also a grand lounge with a (very) grand piano, where you can sip coffee and speculate about which famous guests might have had a tinkle on the old ivories. Acts as diverse as Anna Pavlova, Noel Coward, Peter Kay and The Stylistics have all played at the Opera House, so this hotel must have seen its fair share of celebrities since Mary Queen of Scots tippled here.

From the hotel's Theatre Bar you look out onto The Crescent, a gorgeous Grade I listed Georgian pile which, as the name suggests, is crescent shaped. Unfortunately, this architectural gem, complete with Roman baths, has been at the centre of neglect and legal wrangling for years, leaving it surrounded with ugly safety fencing. Apparently, some deal has now been done between various 'responsible' organisations to turn it into a 5-star hotel and thermal spa. Let us hope that this brings to an end a frankly shameful chapter in the history of a building of national importance.

Without the efforts of the Dukes of Devonshire to develop it as a spa Buxton would probably have remained a fairly ordinary Pennine market town. The desire to make it a rival to Bath though, in the 17th and 18th centuries, was not entirely thought through properly because, basically, Buxton is too flipping cold for people trying to convalesce. At 1,000 ft. it is the highest town in England, which means tons of snow in winter and hills that make great ski runs for wheelchairs. You do still see genteel, elderly ladies in bath-chairs, sipping tea in the elegant hotels, but I doubt whether they are here for the waters.

We left the hotel to see another favourite Devonshire edifice, an improbably fantastical construct bearing similarities to Brighton Pavilion, or The Taj Mahal. It used to be The Royal Devonshire Hospital but now it forms part of The University of Derby. It is a circular building with a gigantic central dome, flanked by lesser domes and minarets. The central dome is so huge, at 44 metres in diameter, that it is bigger than the Pantheon in Rome and St. Mark's Basilica! You might think that it must have been a cathedral or a palace but, actually, it was originally a mews for the horses of the 5th Duke. In other words it was a giant stables, capable of accommodating more than one hundred horses. The central atrium is big enough to exercise a horse at full gallop, and when they had finished their training they were led into enormous stalls, which emanate from the dome like spokes on some great wheel. These same stables became wards during the time of the building's stint as a hospital.

The dome is so high that a pendulum has been suspended from the very apex reaching all the way to the floor, in order to conduct a scientific experiment. This is the 'Foucault Pendulum' (no, I don't know how to pronounce it). It moves gently as you watch and by doing so it is (amazingly) demonstrating the rotation of the earth.

One more bit of fun to be had in the dome is to stand in the centre and cough or clap. The building echoes the sound round and round, much to the irritation of the uniformed attendants - and then you might have to 'leg it', which also makes a great echo.

Buxton marks the transition from the White Peak to the Dark Peak. Hereon in, to the north, the millstone grit has the upper hand and, being much less subject to water erosion than limestone, it is typified by rounder hills, moorland and dark stone walls. Directly east of Buxton is the way to Chatsworth, the centre of the dukedom, and the route dips in and out of white and dark peaks, but always following the same pattern – a drive up a steep hill followed by a descent into some beautiful river valley.

The Hope Valley is one of the most beautiful in this part of the Peak District. At the western end stands Mam Tor, which means 'Mother Hill', and like a watchful mother it makes its presence felt along the whole length of the valley. Mam Tor is also known as 'Shivering Mountain' because it is so unstable that over the years the main A525, which runs at the foot of it, repeatedly collapsed until eventually it had to be abandoned altogether. Now, the only way down to the valley bottom is via a horrendously steep and dramatic minor road called 'Winnats Pass'. You can still walk along the old road. The tarmac is mostly intact and you can even follow the white lines but every now and then the road surface drops several feet or just falls away entirely. These are not the sort of pot-holes you want to drive over!

Just before you plunge down Winnats Pass there are a couple of less well known attractions in the area of Mam Tor. The first is Giants Hole Cave, which is at a farm below Rushup Edge. It is probably the oldest lead mine in the country, dating to pre- Roman times. Giants Hole forms part of a network of caves and caverns around Castleton and it is noted for its stalagmites and stalactites. You pay the farmer £3 to have a look and then descend a metal-rung ladder, before submerging yourself in a sump of water. I couldn't wait!

I was going to go in until I read a rather off-putting description of the place by one intrepid caver, who talked about the cave being well decorated with speleothems, squeezes, crawls, cascades and ducks.

What on earth are speleothems? I imagine them as being similar to velociraptors (and what are ducks doing down there?). I decided that I could do without the excitement.

The other notable curiosity is the old oil well. Yes, 'there's oil in them thar hills!' There are deposits of crude oil under parts of the Pennines and this area is one of them. Sadly, the well has been capped for some time but in the old days Derbyshire folk used to baptise their babies in the oil to bring them good luck - and to waterproof them!

You certainly do need weatherproofing at times up here. I have travelled this way in all weather conditions because I used to commute from Manchester to Sheffield for a number of years. When I took the job in Sheffield there had been a sustained period of mild winters and I figured that with global warming and so on it might not now be such a bad journey. However, from 2004 onwards we seemed to enter a mini ice-age, which made for some interesting weather on the tops of the hills. From where we lived it was a distance of about thirty miles, across the full breadth of the Pennines, and took in some spectacular scenery. On a good day I could do it in less than fifty minutes but in challenging conditions it could take one to two hours, or not even be achievable at all. Many's the day when I have stopped at the top of Winnats Pass, with my heart in my mouth, wondering whether I dare descend this insanely steep, twisting track, over ice and snow so deep that you couldn't work out where the road ended and the moor began. It was not unknown to see a car upside down on its roof as you went down. Further excitement was often provided by sheep that wandered freely around and about and who thought nothing of lying down in the middle of the road. Occasionally they would stand inside the gritting box at the road-side and jump out in front of you at the last moment. I think they liked licking the salt in the box.

Sometimes a nice human moment would occur in such conditions, when groups of anxious commuters gathered at the top of the pass to encourage one another and swap ideas about the best route round. 'Auntie' performs pretty well in snow because she has tall, thin tyres which keep her high off the ground. I carried a shovel and a bag of rock-salt in the boot and more than once I stopped to help out flailing BMWs and the like.

Revisiting this place after some time I fancied a walk up Mam Tor before descending to Castleton. Jane was doubtful of the plan because a wind was 'getting up'. However, I brushed her objections aside and strode off energetically to ascend the summit, which is a twenty minute climb. Jane followed, somewhat reluctantly. The 'Mother Hill' is a Bronze Age fort dating from around 1,200BC and the foundations are still visible. I suppose it was chosen because it is a great vantage point from which to see approaching enemies and it would be an easy point to defend. From the Trig Point looking east towards Sheffield is The Great Ridge, with its twin peaks of Lose Hill and Win Hill. The names of these peaks are said to derive from an ancient Anglo-Saxon battle but, disappointingly, it may be that Win Hill is from the Old English word 'win', meaning 'a pig sty'.

I am not sure how long it took me to realise that Jane was no longer with me. She had been right, the wind was a tad brisk, to say the least, and by the time I reached the top I had to lean into it at practically forty-five degrees. It was then that I noticed an ant-like creature some way below me on all fours, clinging for dear life to a rock.

In the bracing wind the grass looked so inviting waving to and fro, with the sun glistening on its surface. I remembered the Vikings and fancied myself as a brave and rugged mountain man.

'Wouldn't it be fun to roll down the hill rather than walk,' said a voice in my head, 'and so much quicker to get to Jane to rescue her?'

Another voice in my head told me not to be stupid, but I was on fire! Blithely ignoring the boring, urbane voice I lowered myself onto the grass and gingerly let go. I was a gay dog!

On reflection it wasn't one of my better ideas. I suppose it had been forty years since I had last done a 'roly-poly' on a slope. This wasn't just a slope however, it was an increasingly steep descent of hundreds of feet to the floor of the valley. At first I revelled in the sense of freedom as the skies and the hills turned topsy-turvy in my field of vision. The grass was like a carpet and the scent of the wild flowers was in my nostrils. Strains from The Sound of Music drifted through my head once more. Soon though, it wasn't just the scent of the wild flowers that was in my nostrils, but the flowers themselves, and the grass - in my nostrils, mouth, ears, and other sundry orifices. I can't quite recall the exact moment when my sense of euphoria turned to one of horror. I think it was when the sky and the grass began to blur into a single image as my speed increased under the effects of gravity, and The Sound of Music turned into The Ride of the Valkyries.

Fortunately, I hit a rock. It hurt when I hit this rock and I wanted to scream, but I couldn't, because my mouth was full of grass. At least I had stopped. I rolled over painfully to look up and there was Jane, still clinging to the same rock.

"Well," she shouted, above the wind, "I'm glad that you could join me."

I am really not cut out to be a Viking.

If you do manage to make it to the bottom of the Winnats Pass, by whatever method, then you are rewarded with the village of Castleton, which has been a place of importance since Roman times. It has an appropriate castle, at an elevation that allows a watchful presence along the valley, and several caverns and cave systems. In addition to lead Blue John was mined round here, a semi-precious stone unique to this area. Mostly, this blue/yellow fluorspar is made into jewellery but if you visit Vernon Park Museum in Stockport you can find large pots and bowls made of it, and even an amazing, translucent Blue John window.

You can descend the mines and caverns in Castleton if you are brave enough. After Giants Cave the most exciting one is probably Speedwell Cavern. This one has to be negotiated by boat and plucky tourists are required to lie on their backs and propel the craft by pushing on the cavern roof with their feet. It beats 'Alton Towers' any day.

We checked in at 'The Olde Nag's Head'. This had been my favourite pub in Castleton when I travelled home this way from work. It is several hundred years old and used to have an interior to match, with a cast-iron range and oak settles. It was cosy, charming and intimate and cheered weary travellers pausing on their journey. It was just as a pub should be but you notice that I am using the past tense. Now, it seemed that some bright spark had had a good idea to 'modernise' the place. They had ripped out the settles, ripped out the ancient range and tried to make the place more 'open-plan'. To add insult to injury they had replaced the ancient range with a modern, imitation one. The only satisfaction I receive from this tragic process is that whoever fitted the new range has failed to allow the chimney to draw properly, thus ensuring that there is always a great cloud of smoke drifting round the inside of the pub.

I complained bitterly about these changes but the staff just looked at me as if I was daft. Aside from this pub there are several others in Castleton which have also been gutted and filleted, like 'The Castle Hotel' with its 'covered up' Jacobean staircase. Despite all this there remain many fine buildings in the village. In addition to Peveril Castle there is Castleton Hall, which dates from the 17th century and which is now a Youth Hostel. Also, you will find the ancient church of St Edmund's, where you can see some beautifully preserved box pews. But, for my money, the most charming features to be found in Castleton are the tiny, stone terraced houses that meander along the banks of the little river. Wander over the bridge that straddles the idle waters, and gaze at the happy ducks, dabbling; it is a gentle pastoral scene - until you look up. Behind the houses loom the gaping jaws of Peak Cavern, the largest cave opening in the British Isles, where the river emerges darkly from some underground kingdom.

To the north you can't miss the mighty escarpment of Mam Tor. Just behind it and to the right you may notice a flat-topped mountain. This is Kinder Scout, which at 2,088ft, is the highest lump of millstone grit in the Peak District. Large areas of it used to be owned by the Dukes of Devonshire but these days most of it is kept for you and me by the National Trust. Before the war it was off-limits to the public, especially during the hunting season, which left the large working class populations of Manchester and Sheffield without anywhere to stretch their legs on a Sunday. After sweating over looms and steel crucibles all week the hills provided a crucial lung to help these people breathe, stifled and choked as they were by living in the smoky cities. To ban them from their Sunday ramble was a sure way to promote frustration and anger.

Things came to a head in 1932 when a large group of ramblers organised a mass trespass on Kinder Scout. They were met by gamekeepers and police, and confrontation was unavoidable. Some 'trespassers' were beaten and some were arrested, subsequently receiving long jail sentences. However, their point had been made and national outrage at the jail sentences followed the media coverage of the story. Eventually, this resulted in large parts of the mountain being made accessible and sowed the seed for the formation of the Peak District as Britain's first national park. The current Duke has apologised for the way his forbears behaved and indeed now welcomes people to, as he puts it, "share my back garden."

Climbing to the top of Kinder Scout from this side you have to take a very steep gully called 'Jacob's Ladder'. If you recognise that particular biblical reference you will know that it includes a passage where Jacob wrestles all night with the Angel of the

Lord. By the time you get to the top of the mountain you certainly realise the appropriateness of this analogy.

Walking about on the top of Kinder is a bit like being an ant trying to negotiate a Christmas pudding. The whole thing is a giant peat bog and completely featureless. Many planes have crashed up here (over sixty in the Peak District as a whole) due to the fast changing weather conditions, giving it the unenviable title of 'aircraft graveyard'. One of the worst was in 1948 when a USAAF B-29 bomber, of the sort that had dropped the nuclear bomb on Hiroshima, crashed on a routine mission, carrying nothing more deadly than supplies and post. The plane was nicknamed 'Over-exposed', due to the reputation of its reconnaissance photographer, and it had a picture of a nude blonde on the side. The flight path had taken her over Kinder but, because of bad visibility, she was 100ft lower than necessary to clear the peak. 'Over-exposed' was travelling from Scampton in Lincolnshire to the US airbase at Burtonwood near Warrington. The crew had been due to return to the States three days later but, sadly, none survived. There is a dignified memorial marking the site of the crash but, more eerily, because of the preservative nature of the peat, parts of the plane are still visible more than sixty years after the tragedy. Bits of fuselage still flap around in the wind and twisted metal can be found scattered over a wide area.

It is not easy to find the wreck site because everywhere looks so similar on the high plateau that is the summit of Kinder and some might scoff that only a fool would wander around up there to do so, particularly in the middle of winter. Lots of folk do it however, and I well remember of a friend of mine who I snapped in typical 'mad dogs and Englishmen' mode near the top of the mountain, comfortably reading a newspaper in a blizzard!

Chapter 7
Beyond Hope

The following day we paid our dues at the 'Nag' (me still grumbling and muttering) and headed east, taking us ever closer to the Chatsworth estate. The next village you happen upon is Hope, after which the valley is named. This is the site of an enormous cement works and quarry, which produces in excess of 750,000 tons of cement every year. It is slap bang in the middle of the Peak District National Park, in a location that must have been one of the most beautiful in the whole of the Pennine Chain. It was built in 1929, before there was any thought of preserving such lovely places, and remains working to the present day, with its own railway line to move the stone and cement around the country.

I have a theory about this being the inspiration for Saruman's Tower of Orthanc in J.R.R. Tolkien's 'Lord of the Rings'. Consider that Tolkien was a professor at Leeds University in the early 1920s and that he and his wife loved walking in various parts of the Pennines. Is it too much to speculate that on some walking holiday around the Hope Valley he came across construction work on this concrete monstrosity, which soars into the air like some ugly, tiered wedding cake, topped by a chimney that fumes blackly? It reminds me so much of the way in which Saruman despoils his beautiful valley of Isengard, ripping out trees and blasting and torturing the very hills themselves.

I cannot pretend that all of the Pennine Chain is free from industries such as quarrying and cement works but they are few and far between and mostly discreet. I heard one statistic to suggest that if all the stone quarried from Derbyshire in any one year, taken for building work, hardcore etc., were taken from Hampshire instead, it would reduce the level of that county by one metre in height over its entire area.

Chatsworth lies just a little south and east of here, past the unfortunately named hamlet of Shatton and close to the 'plague village' of Eyam. But before we leave the Hope Valley I must relate a little story from the period I worked at a school in Sheffield, when I had cause to pass through Hope every day. If you are travelling from Sheffield to Buxton then the sequence of villages westwards goes: Hathersage, Bamford, Hope, and then Castleton. It was that time of year when the wearisome task of writing reports fell upon the staff. It is not unusual for teachers to go slightly mad at such times, having been worked to the point of distraction. On this particular occasion the headmaster came rushing into the staff-room looking perplexed and agitated, waving a piece of paper in his hand.

"Mr Wright," he ejaculated, to an elderly teacher slumped in an armchair at break time, "I simply do not understand your comment on this boy's mathematics report. You have merely written the word 'Castleton'! What can this mean?" The teacher thus addressed, an old hand at the reports game, looked up sanguinely from his cup of tea and replied sadly,

"Beyond hope Headmaster…!"

The approach to Chatsworth is an impressive one whichever direction you choose. We were approaching from Baslow and the first intimation that the great estate was upon us came at the village of Edensor. Edensor looks rather stage-managed and twee, as though it has been placed where it is with great exactitude – which it has. In the 18th century it was demolished and moved to where it is now, lock, stock and barrel, because in its original location it was spoiling the view for the contemporaneous Duchess!

Drive round a slight bend in the road and then catch your breath as Chatsworth is glimpsed. It really is situated pleasantly in the Derwent Valley. The first house on this lovely spot by the River Derwent was the brainchild of Bess of Hardwicke, the redoubtable wife of William Cavendish, and begun in 1553. The valley is wide and fertile and it gives way to woods and then to moorland above. The air is gentle in the valley and 'recommends itself to the senses', but on the old maps of Chatsworth the surrounding moors are referred to as 'a wild and howling place'. The earliest known settler in this place was a Viking called Chetel, who had joint ownership with a Saxon lord. The Normans took control of it after 1066 and the area doesn't really come to prominence again until it is bought by Bess and William Cavendish, in 1549.

We turned into the drive, over a little bridge and past an 18th century folly. Sheep grazed on the open land and, in the far distance, the Emperor Fountain could be seen thrusting heavenward over the tops of the trees. The Cavendish family are very lucky to live here.

William Cavendish was a courtier or civil servant in the reign of Henry VIII. He was a member of the Court of Augmentation, the body that disposed of the lands of the monasteries after their dissolution. Between 1536 and 1540 the number of monasteries in England went from 800 to nil and William, by luck or good judgement, managed to acquire lands around what is now Chatsworth, as well as Bolton Abbey in Yorkshire. The family's star was definitely in the ascendancy and it rocketed through space when William married the formidable Bess. She was an ambitious and talented lady who retained pretensions to place one of her descendants on the throne of England. She persuaded William to leave the South of England and move to her native Derbyshire, no doubt to make him more malleable!

Their success was assured when in 1694 a later Cavendish, also called William, was made 1st Duke of Devonshire for his part in helping the Protestant William of Orange overthrow the Catholic James II as King of England. They gained more land and property by this and haven't really looked back since, although crippling death duties in 1950 forced the family to sell Hardwicke Hall, Bess's old house. It is now looked after by the National Trust.

'Auntie' felt as if she was coming home as I parked her at the side of the house. Hens pecked languidly around the parked cars, which gave the place a delightful air of English eccentricity and we alighted regally to consider this great ancestral pile of the Dukes of Devonshire. There is some mystery as to why the title of 'Devonshire' was given to the 1st Duke when his lands were largely in Derbyshire. There is a suggestion that it was a simple clerical error and that someone wrote 'Devonshire' by mistake. I suppose such things happen when human ambition is thwarted by indifferent bureaucracy, or maybe the clerk had never heard of Derbyshire as it is north of the Watford Gap! Either way you probably wouldn't want to complain to Henry VIII.

Chatsworth House has been altered and extended over the years. Bess of Hardwicke finished the Elizabethan house in the 1560s and it occupied the same footprint as the main block of the current house, with dimensions of about 190ft by 170ft. In 1687 the 4th Duke started to remodel the whole place, although the south façade retains its Elizabethan style. The finest designers were brought in and the West (front) façade became a triumph of Baroque architecture, to rival the royal residences at Greenwich and the palaces of Paris and Rome. The nine bays, flanked by ionic pilasters, culminate in a centrepiece which has four great columns rising from a pediment to an apex. The many windows have frames coated with gold leaf, which catch the setting sun and light up the whole of the façade. It started out as a satisfyingly symmetrical place overlooking the River Derwent. However, various wings and towers were added on by different dukes and, to my mind, the place doesn't look as attractive as say Vanbrugh's Castle Howard, in North Yorkshire.

We decided to visit the great gardens first. Designed by Capability Brown the formal parts of the garden flow into and blend with the natural landscape of the Derwent Valley. There happened to be a sculpture exhibition in situ, with some amazing works on display by such high-powered artists as Barbara Hepworth, Anthony Gormley and even Rodin. Aesthetically speaking my favourite was the Rodin although, at some more basic level, I was attracted to the sculpture of a giant, nude Kate Moss! Apart from these the statues I remember best were the classical figures on pedestals which line the walk immediately behind the house. They all resembled Olympians in differing manly poses, naked except for a modest fig leaf over delicate parts. As we stood looking at them a little girl walked past with her parents and she stopped and stared at the semi-nude bodies curiously.

"Daddy," she articulated finally, after long study, "Why are those men wearing crabs on their bottoms?"

If you are out to 'keep up with the Jones's' then you haven't a hope if you are next-door neighbours of the Devonshires. Their total estates run to over 70,000 acres and include properties in London, Ireland and Yorkshire. I suppose these are merely holiday homes compared to the main house in Derbyshire.

Whatever you may possess, Chatsworth has a bigger, better version of it.

If water features 'float your boat' (literally) then Chatsworth has a full-size lake to see. It is fed by water collected in an eight acre hole, dug out especially for the purpose on the moors above. Out of the lake rises the Emperor Fountain to a height of 296 ft., the highest in the world when it was installed, in 1832. It is entirely gravity powered and employed ground-breaking engineering for its time.

There are smaller and more intricate fountains such as the Willow Tree Fountain, which looks just like a tree but can cascade water on the unsuspecting observer. There is the Sea-Horse Fountain and also one that looks like a giant, metallic chocolate-orange. At regular intervals it rises, like a surfacing submarine from a large pond, and opens up into spurting segments.

If glasshouses 'do it' for you then Chatsworth has some prime examples to drool over, including an enormous orangery and various hothouses dedicated to growing giant Amazonian lilies. In 1836 The Great Conservatory was constructed which (naturally) was the biggest in the world. It was so big that it had a carriageway through the middle of it and caused one visitor, a Mr W. Adam, to comment (with somewhat confused imagery) that it was:

"... a mountain of glass, an unexampled structure, a sea of glass, when the waves are settling down after a storm."

Certainly, if one lived in it then one could safely throw stones. Sadly, this particular building was demolished in 1920 but there are plenty of others remaining that look pretty impressive. I bet there are undiscovered species of flora and fauna wandering around in them and I for one would not like to be left alone inside after dark.

The gardens can boast a maze, a terraced cascade, a stupendous rockery (which must have used half the annual output from Derbyshire's stone quarries), a farm, a hunting lodge and formal parterres. We set about exploring as much as we could and Meg particularly enjoyed the terraced cascade. People were paddling in it and Jane threw a stick into it for Meg. Unfortunately, as she did so for the umpteenth time she slipped and fell headlong into the water. In my hurry to help her out I slipped on the muddy grass and we both floundered around in the dirt for a while before we managed to regain an upright position.

I don't think it would have been so bad except that a few moments later we happened to bump into the Duke and Duchess, who were showing some important guests round the garden (perhaps minor royals from Albania or equivalent). At the sight of our sorry selves the aristocratic voices trailed away, the noble expressions frozen on their ducal faces and they regarded us with undisguised horror. If I had still had a forelock to tug then I would have, but instead we simply grinned stupidly and shuffled off sideways, as though we had been let out for the day from some local institution.

Any local institution may well be a charitable enterprise of the Cavendish family. They have been at the centre of local, and indeed national, life for generations. They have served in high offices of state and also with distinction in the military. The first son of the 10th Duke died on active service in WWII and the second son, who became the 11th Duke, won the Military Cross for bravery.

On a slightly lighter note I like the story about the 10th Duke who, during the war, was visited by an official from the War Office to see what manpower the Chatsworth estate might spare, in order to assist the war effort. After conducting his survey the official made his report to the duke.

"Your Grace," he began, "I fully understand why an estate of this magnitude requires seventy gardeners and under-gardeners, fifty footmen, grooms and stable-boys, ninety servants and butlers, maids and ladies of the bed-chamber, head chefs, sous-chefs, chefs de partie, and commis chefs - but is there really any necessity for *two* pastry chefs?"

To which His Grace is supposed to have replied, "Damn it! Can't a man enjoy a biscuit?"

There is a comfortable feeling of affluence generated under the wing of the Cavendish family. Their presence is demonstrated by many grand buildings and by the beautifully manicured pasture land extending for miles around Chatsworth. One way of measuring their influence is to note how far and wide you see pubs with the name 'Devonshire Arms'.

Somehow Jane and I managed to dry off and clean up in the toilets, enough to be let into the house, for a small fee. Chatsworth House is well worth the tour although, being privately owned, it is somewhat different to your average National Trust property. You get used to modestly furnished or even bare rooms in a NT country house or castle, but Chatsworth is stuffed to the gills with priceless paintings, furniture, ornaments and tapestries. This takes some doing because there are one hundred and twenty-six rooms to fill.

A Damien Hirst sculpture, 'The Exquisite Pain of St. Bartholomew' seemed rather squeezed in at the foot of the main Palladian staircase. This statue represents the unfortunate St Bartholomew, standing with outstretched arm, over which hangs his entire flayed skin. The difficulty is, the way it has been sited it could easily be mistaken for a coat stand, and the poor saint might end up with the odd anorak draped over his arm, just to add to his problems.

This overcrowding continues all the way round. Lucian Freud paintings fight for wall-space with old masters, behind Ming vases, standing atop Chippendale tables. Apparently, the Chatsworth carpenters have to be able to work in forty different styles when it comes to repairing or restoring the place. If I didn't know any better I would say that it is just a tad ostentatious. I hate to think what the home insurance premium might be.

Improbably, we happened to bump into the duke again. The family's private apartments are situated on the southeast of the building and visitors are normally steered away from that area by a polite guide, of the sort you normally see following foreign journalists round North Korea. In this instance the guide had deserted his post temporarily and, lacking direction for the tour, we just wandered along a corridor and were about to turn right through a door when out flew a bewildered looking visitor having his hand warmly shaken by the 12th Duke of Devonshire. It all happened in a flash - one minute there was His Grace wishing us all well and promising to see us later, and then he backed up quickly and shut the door, like a clam retreating into its shell. A few moments later an embarrassed guide came puffing up the hallway and ushered us away from the area, hastily replacing an errant rope barrier. I feel as though we are practically on Christmas card terms with the Devonshires these days.

Chapter 8
Green City Noir

'Tha can allus tell a Yorkshireman,
but tha can't tell him much.'

Noir: Suggestive of danger or violence;
tough characters; bleak settings.

Sheffield, June, 2007

The rocks tumble down the hillside and onto the road, some of them the size of small boulders. They become part of the detritus being washed along towards the bridge at the bottom. No longer can the road be recognised as such; it more resembles a river as normally tame springs and streams spout forcefully off the banks at the side. The rain pounds down on the car roof as the ancient wipers do their best to cope with the rivulets of water pouring down the windscreen. The sky looks angry - acid-green and black. I glance in the rear-view mirror and see a police car following me. As we approach the bridge it pulls sideways across the road, effectively blocking it. The police are stopping traffic behind me. It is too dangerous to carry on but I have no alternative - there is no way back for me.

After leaving Chatsworth Jane and I were on our way to the second wedding of our trip, that of an ex-colleague of mine, from the time I worked in Sheffield. Being so close to the city set off a whole chain of reminiscences about the place, starting with the day the rains came.

The passage above is the best way I could think of to convey the impact upon me of the great floods of June 25th 2007. The floods came unexpectedly and had profound consequences for the city of Sheffield, which lies north east of Chatsworth, on the eastern edge of the Pennines. Altogether, June 25th was a very 'Noir' date indeed!

Although it had been raining steadily for most of the day people expected it to slacken off. Instead, the rain fell harder and harder until the water in the gutters began to spread across roads and pavements. I had a thirty mile journey over the tops of the Pennines and I knew that whatever the weather was doing here it would be ten times worse on the high passes around Strines Moor and Rushup Edge. I left the meeting I was in fairly 'sharpish', muttering my apologies, because I sensed that I had to go - straightaway!

Immediately, it became obvious that this was going to be no ordinary or simple journey home. Already there were tree branches, stones and earth washed onto and along the streets. I remembered the story about the dams above Sheffield that had collapsed in 1864, in similar conditions, killing hundreds. I was heading for those dams. Now I found myself leaving behind the police car and heading towards the notorious Snake Pass. Perhaps I had panicked but I reasoned that Sheffield was not going to be a comfortable place to stay in that night.

At least I got that right. I didn't know it but as I was heading out of town the centre was being overwhelmed by floodwaters. Kelham Island, a low-lying industrial area (home to the famous 'Kelham Island Brewery') was sinking under several feet of fast-moving floods. Houses, motorways and businesses were all being threatened by the swollen waters of the five rivers that flow through Sheffield.

More importantly, lives were being put at risk. It would be later that week before stories started to emerge of the carnage taking place at this moment. A colleague of mine had arranged to meet her friend in town after work and was concerned that she had not heard from her. Ringing her mobile she asked her where she was.

"I am in a traffic jam," came the reply.

"Whereabouts?" asked my colleague.

"Well, we have just floated past the Co-op," was the extraordinary answer.

Lots of factories, businesses and peoples' homes were affected that day; indeed, the award-winning 'Kelham Island Brewery' took two years to recover.

I had decided to carry on so, losing the police car in my wake, I took a deep breath and prepared to ford the bridge ahead. This normally peaceful little crossing point of the River Rivelin now had the river-waters flowing right over it in frothing, angry surges. The question was how deep was the flood? Fortunately, 'Auntie's' legendary high ground clearance came to my rescue. I had been through deep waters in her before and she had always survived because the exhaust is high off the floor and the car's electrics are sited far away from the radiator grille. In other words she is well designed! Gingerly, I inched forward into the raging torrent, which rose at least halfway up the door of the car at the deepest spot. It was 'wing and a prayer' time but 'Auntie' ploughed on and the waters parted. Somehow I made it to the other side, still dry and able to contemplate the horrors of the Snake Pass and beyond.

The rest of that journey home remains a bit of a blur (probably because I was unable to see properly out of the windscreen). The only other lasting memory was reaching Ladybower Reservoir and hearing and seeing water thundering into it from every conceivable angle on the surrounding hills, as if a giant were filling an enormous bath with not one, but many taps!

What I really needed was not a car with a Viking badge but a Viking longship. Failing that I would have settled for a Sheffield Viking. What about Sean Bean? One has only to look at the Sheffield actor playing Boromir in 'Lord of the Rings', to see that he is a Viking. The square jaw, blond hair and piercing blue eyes shout out that he is a Norseman! You cannot imagine Sean failing at any feat of physical prowess and valour. He could have waded through the floods towing my car!

How surprising then to realise that Sheffield may be the line at which the Vikings were eventually stopped on their migration south. Sheffield has been mooted as the site of one of the great Viking battles in England, the Battle of Brunanburh, in 937AD (although other places also claim their patch as the location). It would make sense though for Sheffield to be the place. According to the Anglo-Saxon Chronicle, at Brunanburh, 'There was put to flight the Northmen Chief'.

England made a major step towards identity by winning this battle, in which the Saxon King Athelstan defeated an alliance of Gaels, Norsemen and Picts. The battle is recorded in many medieval chronicles and was referred to at the time as 'The Great War'. Probably it was the first occasion a rigid dividing line between north and south was drawn up. To this day anything south of Sheffield is regarded as passing from The North into The Midlands. Sheffielders still occasionally refer to Lincolnshire people as being 'Lincolnshire Yellow-Bellies'.

Whether or not the battle was fought in Sheffield, it was certainly a very bloody affair, in which five kings and seven earls were killed. It is fascinating to read a description of the aftermath of the battle from Aethelweard's Chronicle:

'Then the dark raven with horned beak,
And the livid toad, the eagle and the kite,
The hound and the wolf in mottled hue,
Were long refreshed by these delicacies.
In this land no greater war was ever waged,
Nor did such a slaughter ever surpass that one'.

These days Sheffield is largely a very pleasant and civilised place with a cosmopolitan population. Certainly it has some scruffy parts but it is also blessed with a first-class university, an excellent teaching hospital and many fine Victorian stone properties. They are set in leafy suburbs like Broomhill, which was once described by John Betjeman as 'the prettiest in England', in 'The Shell Guide to Britain'. It has the City Hall for concerts, two main theatres, four museums, an art gallery and attractive Botanical Gardens.

Sheffield is famously known as 'Steel City' because of its world importance in the production of iron and steel. However, locals call it 'The Green City' because they claim you can see green hills from whichever part of town you happen to be in. Also, they sometimes refer to it as 'the biggest village in the world' because it has such a friendly, communal atmosphere. I don't think this means that people wave to complete strangers from the top decks of buses or engage them in intimate discussions on the streets but there does exist a type of cheerful banter in the shops and public buildings, a sort of recognised consensus that people look out for each other and take a pride in their city.

This is definitely a Yorkshire characteristic and we must now remember that we have tiptoed over the Derbyshire border into God's own county! Here we reach the limits of 'duck' country and enter 'love' country. 'Are you alright duck/love?' Some may call it the land of the stiff-necked people, but I think that Pennine Yorkshire is merely the rest of the North writ large (with the possible exception of the Geordies). As the Pennines rise, like peaks on a graph, so the character of the people reaches extremes and exaggerations, and calmer more reasoned counsels are made to seem insipid. The counties surrounding the Pennines, with quiet uneventful countryside, seem to live under the shadow of the peaks, literally and metaphorically. In my experience Lincolnshire folk are shy and retiring, as are Staffordshire folk, whilst Cheshire is like a bit of the Home Counties transplanted into the North. What is to a Pennine person good natured banter might be construed as rude and uncouth to a lowland dweller. Whilst the poem Desiderata may have achieved widespread popularity in the 1970s, exhorting us to 'Go calmly amidst the noise and haste and remember what peace there may be in silence', Pennine men have for years been considering the old verse, 'A Yorkshireman's Advice to His Son':

'Hear all, see all, say nowt (nothing)
Eat all, drink all, pay nowt.
And if tha ever does owt (anything) for nowt,
Do it for thisen (yourself)'

Much more down to earth don't you think? Rumour has it that it is being adopted by the banks!

Sheffield lies on the eastern edge of the South Pennines, in the same way that Manchester lies just to the west of them, on the same latitude. The strange thing is that the two cities don't have much communication with each other. They might as well be three thousand miles apart and not thirty. There is no proper road link unless you go absolutely miles around, and the direct routes, such as the Snake Pass, are at the mercy of the elements. If you ever listen to the weather forecast note the frequency in which this infamous pass is announced as being closed, usually buried under ten feet of snow (and that's just in the summer!). You can try the journey by train which, although spectacular, is not for the faint-hearted due to the extraordinarily lengthy periods spent travelling under mountains, and in any case the tiny two-carriage train service stops at 8.30pm. It is as if the two cities are being held apart by supernatural powers.

Of course it is the Pennines that are to blame; merely thirty miles or so across at this point and yet capable of developing communities so dissimilar and antagonistic to each other that it caused the 'Wars of the Roses'! I jest - partly. There is, as I have already mentioned, a real sense of Yorkshire Pride in Sheffield. In fact, Yorkshire as a whole is a really self-confident county, unaffected by what others may think of it. It hosts a 'Yorkshireman of the Year' ceremony and has an award for being a 'Yorkshire Icon'. What other counties do that? And yet it remains intensely patriotic. You see a lot of Union flags flying in Yorkshire, and Sheffield is no exception, despite its one-time reputation for being 'The People's Republic'.

Of course being a centre for both the steel industry and the silver trade has rightly engendered local pride in the city of Sheffield. If you ever tour round a steelworks then you begin to realise how tough the workers must be to work in such conditions. The heat, the noise, the dangers from molten steel and gigantic crucibles cannot fail to impress, and all these contained in buildings so large that they could accommodate several cathedrals without any trouble; so big in fact that some of them had to take into account the curvature of the earth as part of their design!

From the steel and the silver came cutlery; so much so that the name of Sheffield became synonymous with cutlery. Sheffield does not only have a Lord Mayor like most major cities but it also has a Master Cutler, whose grand title was awarded by Act of Parliament in 1624. His or her duties are now largely ceremonial, as not so much cutlery is manufactured hereabouts as it once was, but I can vividly remember an official dinner I attended in Sheffield, shortly after I started working in the city. The first thing that most of the guests did, when seated at the beautifully-laid tables, was to pick up the cutlery and examine it, like master craftsmen. They balanced a fork on the fulcrum of a finger to test its weight distribution or they held a knife at arms length and squinted at it to see if it was straight, and they breathed on spoons and polished them on their sleeves so as to better observe the quality of the finish. I was impressed and contemplated spitting on a side knife and rubbing it on my trousers - but some instinct stopped me.

Steel has had another effect on modern Sheffield, in the form of the Crucible Theatre. Based on the shape of the crucibles used to smelt iron, the theatre is a triumph of stage design. It manages to remain intimate whilst having a grand stage and a large auditorium, raking upwards on three sides of a circle, just like an arena theatre of Ancient Greece. It has excellent production values and I spent many a happy evening there as a member of the audience and also, on one sublime occasion, as director.

I suppose that one of the most unusual things that happened to me connected to the Crucible Theatre was the curious incident of the corpse in the car. I had been directing a production of 'Loot' by Joe Orton and, if you are familiar with the play, you will know that it requires a prop corpse. You would be amazed how difficult it is to get one! In the end I rang up the Crucible and asked them. Yes, they did have a prop corpse and yes, we were welcome to borrow it, so I arranged to collect it.

Taking a colleague to help I subsequently arrived at the stage door to pick up the 'body' and prepared to put it in my car. There were two things wrong with this plan. The first was that it was too big to fit in the boot and so it was with some difficulty that we managed to wedge it in the cabin, with its feet on the dashboard and its head on the rear windowsill. This might have been alright with a mannequin or a puppet but the other problem was that this 'corpse' looked so realistic. Of course, it had been used on the professional stage and it had to appear genuine. However, it was so effective that as we drove through Sheffield we began to get startled reactions from passers-by. This wouldn't have been so bad if my colleague hadn't waved and smiled at everybody, especially the police. I had visions of starting a helicopter manhunt but, fortunately, the police weren't as stupid as we were and a quick check reassured them that we weren't body snatchers.

The Crucible stands in Tudor Square next to the Lyceum, an attractive Victorian theatre. On the other side of the square stands the Winter Gardens which is an interesting mixture of a hothouse and a shopping centre. And just round the corner from the Winter Gardens is one of the best pubs in Sheffield - 'The Brown Bear'. If you like your city centre pubs traditional then 'The Brown Bear' is the place. Its regulars are like characters from some period drama. It has the 19th century working class husband, boozing away his family's wages, and it has the abused wife, shouting through the open window for her man to come home and not to spend all his wages on drink. It has the 11.00am through to 11.00pm customers, swatting imaginary flies, but it also has an assortment of business and professional people, traders and theatre types, all rubbing shoulders together. It doesn't do food, hasn't been re-modelled and sells beer for little more than £1. Perfect.

Sheffield pride extends into unexpected areas. For example, it has loads of its own food products very similar to nationally known ones, such as Henderson's Relish, which is very like Worcestershire Sauce, or the Sheffield Cobbler, which to me tastes like any other cobbler (but try saying that to a local!). The word Yorkshire seems to convey honesty, robustness and quality, which is somewhat at odds with the supposed reputation of Yorkshiremen for being mean and forthright. Yorkshire itself lends its name as a prefix to all sorts of products, like Yorkshire Tea or Yorkshire Biscuits. I was once even given Yorkshire Slippers for Christmas. I wear them whenever I sing Yorkshire Carols. 'Yorkshire Carols!' I hear you cry. 'Isn't that going a tad too far?' Well, on the outskirts of Sheffield, in a small village (dubiously named Dungworth), there is a pub where Yorkshire Christmas Carols are sung. They have special words and tunes that are not much known outside Sheffield and North Derbyshire. On the ear the carols sound like you know them, because they are similar to such universal ones as 'While

Shepherds Watch' and so on - but they are uniquely different. Examples of titles include 'Moriah', 'Egypt' and 'Old Foster'. Here is a sample verse from 'A Yorkshire Wassail':

'We've got a little purse,
Made of leathern ratchin skin.
We want a little of your money,
To line it well within'

Even at Christmas money doesn't seem to be far from the Yorkshire mind!

Visitors are welcome on Advent Sundays but you have to understand that the carollers are a genuine bunch - it is not a manufactured event. One film crew got threatened with violence for repeatedly asking that a particular carol be sung again and again, in order to get the perfect 'take'. You might think it odd that carols are sung in pubs but it is true to say that they were often composed and heard there before they were ever heard in churches; the reason being that during the 19th century carols were considered too vernacular and lightweight for parts of the established church.

I don't know whether St John's Church, in the Sheffield suburb of Ranmoor, is one that used to frown upon carols - it certainly would have done if its style of service matched its high and imposing spire. Next to St John's stands 'The Ranmoor Inn' and it was to this pub that 'Clarkie' and I used to retire on Friday evenings after work. Clarkie is a historian and happens to be the President of The Sheffield Historical Association. I once helped him out on a trip he had arranged for the association to visit Lincoln Cathedral, by volunteering to drive the minibus. Even though this was quite a sacrifice for me, being a Saturday, I did it because Clarkie had supported me on several ventures. I drove the thirty miles from where we lived, collected the minibus and picked up the members of the Sheffield Historical Association. Off we set for Lincoln and all appeared to be well.

Now, Clarkie is what you might call a 'bit of a character'. Think of someone with the delivery and gravitas of a Churchill (complete with cigar) and the frame of Martin Johnson, with just a dash of G.K. Chesterton and W.C. Fields thrown in!

After the trip round the cathedral Clarkie approached me frowningly.

"Peter!" he fired at me like a broadside from a warship, dignifying my name with an emphasis normally reserved for great leaders of men.

"I would like to invite you for lunch," he said, with formality and grandeur, and the merest glint in his eye, "*on* the Sheffield Historical Association."

I murmured my deferential approval.

"I know a little place round the corner," he announced. "I'll see you there in fifteen minutes." And he steamed off in the opposite direction, smoking like a Dreadnought.

Duly, I sought out the pub I thought he had meant. I ordered a half pint of mild beer and a small sausage sandwich, as I did not want to impose upon the largesse of the Sheffield Historical Association. I waited patiently, sipping my beer, but Clarkie didn't appear. The sausage sandwich came, small and burnt, but still no Clarkie. Eventually, lunchtime was over and I trudged despondently back to the cathedral for our afternoon talk from the librarian. And there was Clarkie, walking serenely back the way he had left me earlier.

"Where were you Peter?" he queried cheerily. "I have had a forty pound bottle of wine and a splendid meal."

"I waited for you where we arranged," I sulked.

"Nonsense Peter, you must have misunderstood."

My mouth fell open but I said no more. I must admit that I did not listen to the librarian's talk very charitably.

Nevertheless, I cheered up when we returned to Sheffield later that evening. Just a thirty mile drive home now, I thought to myself. But Clarkie was having none of it.

"Peter, you must allow me to make up for lunchtime and get you a meal – on the Sheffield Historical Association."

I demurred, but Clarkie swept all arguments to one side.

"Dear boy, you can get the train! What time is the last train to Manchester?"

"8.35pm."

"Excellent. We have time for a pre-prandial drink whilst we take in the sights!"

He made it sound very agreeable and I did feel that the Sheffield Historical Association still owed me something. I could get the train to work on Monday morning and pick up my car then. It was safely parked.

So, I consented and off we went into Sheffield, with Clarkie pointing out the sights of historical and cultural interest. We passed the hospital, the university, Weston Park and the red-light district. Clarkie was a mine of information! I wasn't quite sure where we would be eating but every time we passed a pub he ushered me in and my hopes rose. The pattern was the same in every pub. Clarkie would stand at the bar and order a 'pre-prandial' drink, whilst waxing lyrical about the ruins of Sheffield Castle or wherever we happened to be. After the drink I would tentatively ask if food was being served, and the answer from the bar staff was always in the negative.

"Never mind!" roared Clarkie, after about our fourth pub, "I am sure that the next one will."

Did I mention that he has Chuchillian appetites when it comes to drinking? I mean, I enjoy a drink as much as the next man but Clarkie is in a league of his own. I felt like a complete amateur next to him. The beer didn't seem to touch the sides of his throat on its way down. When I mentioned to my colleagues on the following Monday that I had been out drinking with

Clarkie there were lots of soft whistles and raised eyebrows. How was I still living they wondered? The point is it seemed not to affect him very much - he just became even louder and more loquacious. I on the other hand, having had an early start to the day, and having driven a minibus full of OAPs to Lincoln and back, and having eaten only a small, burnt sausage sandwich for lunch for my troubles felt, after four pints of beer, somewhat 'squiffy'.

It was two pubs and two more pints of beer later and Clarkie was in full flow. He leant over and addressed me confidentially.

"Peter, did you know that as well as being the President of the Sheffield Historical Association, I am also Secretary of Sheffield Cemetery?"

I was starting to go cross-eyed and slip beneath the level of the bar, but this arresting information made me pause momentarily in my downwards slither.

"Shh-ecretary of Shh-effield Sch-emetery...?" I repeated stupidly.

Clarkie nodded and tapped his nose with one finger.

"If you ever need a second hand coffin then I can get you a good deal."

"Sch-econd-hand...?" I squeaked, thoroughly alarmed.

My fuzzy brain tried to compute this sentence but it kept getting stuck at the words 'second hand'. Why would anyone want a second hand coffin, and worse, how on earth did it *become* second hand? I felt a little ill.

Suddenly Clarkie looked sheepish.

"Remind me Peter, what time was your last train?"

"8.35pm," I answered, my stomach rumbling as my mind surrendered its last thought about a meal, whether or not on the shh-odding Shh-effield Hish-torical Assh-o-sch-ia-shun. Clarkie looked at his watch and then looked glum.

"I think we had better run," he pronounced gravely.

Now, I had no idea which part of Sheffield we were in, or how far it was to the station, but I did see by the clock on the wall of the bar that it was 8.15pm. Assuming this was the correct time we had only twenty minutes before my train left - the final train to Manchester.

In retrospect we could have got a cab. Why didn't we think of that? Maybe it was the six pints of Abbeydale beer we had consumed which, although tasting wonderful, probably didn't facilitate logical thought. What's worse it was raining, and we had no coats. Suddenly panicking, we both rushed out into the rain. Clarkie made an abrupt right and started running up the middle of the road. Why not the pavement? I have no idea. I only remember his shoulders, square under his sports jacket, with the rain bouncing off them as we criss-crossed the city centre, mainly on roads, heading goodness knows where. All I knew was that I had to keep up, or I would probably die.

How long that journey lasted I cannot tell. It became a blur of street lights and pounding pavements, breathing heavily and trying not to choke on rainwater as I inhaled. Actually I *can* tell! It was precisely twenty-one minutes. I know that because I arrived puffing and panting onto the platform just as the last train to Manchester entered the tunnel at the far end, on its way across the Pennines. I collapsed in a gibbering, soggy heap, cursing Clarkie and wishing I had never heard of the Sheffield - etc, etc, etc.

Despondently, I heaved my weary frame back along the platform and into the main thoroughfare of the station, only to see Clarkie, still standing where I had left him, steaming like some bull that had just done several rounds with the matador. Our eyes met, and I think we both knew at that moment that I was finally going to get a meal - on the Sheffield Historical Association!

Chapter 9
The Long and the Short and the Crooked

'Bless them all, bless them all, the long
and the short and the tall'
- WWII song

Chesterfield is a North Midland town and its feel is that of Derbyshire rather than Yorkshire. It is located between Chatsworth and Sheffield and, as it was more or less on the way to our next wedding in Dore, we decided to pay a visit. Chesterfield is most famous for its church, which has an extremely tall, yet crooked spire. Indeed, when you get up close it is twisted to an alarming degree, more resembling a corkscrew than a spire. In fact, it is out of true to the extent of nine feet six inches!

Apparently, what happened is that centuries ago, when the spire was being built, they used unseasoned timber for the frame. This didn't present a problem for many years but eventually the wood started to shrink and warp, resulting in the whole edifice pulling to one side. I bet the bishop was furious - but it was probably a cash job!

Although I had driven past, round and through Chesterfield many times I had never lingered there.

We parked near the station and walked to the market square at the centre of town. I really wasn't expecting the large scale of the market; it was like those continental markets in Leuven or Munich, with a huge number of stalls. Traders were announcing their wares and you could easily fill up on all the free samples of food on offer. There was a real air of bustle and vibrancy about the place.

The greatest find for me was a traditional Victorian pie shop on the edge of the square. It had those lovely, rounded, corner windows at the shop entrance, plus a beautiful mosaic floor and a high ceiling that arched above the old glass counters. Under the glass was the most delicious array of pastries and pies that a boy could wish for. You must remember that we are not so far away from Melton Mowbray here and therefore pork pies are a speciality.

As we ate our pies I had a look at the architecture of the buildings round the market. They are an eclectic mixture of Tudor, Georgian and Victorian but, thank goodness, they have resisted the brutal architectural fashion of the 1960s. We walked past a 12th century pub – 'The Royal Oak', which is in The Shambles area of town, and popped in for a swift half. It had an attached chapel, presumably where pious customers could go to pray between rounds.

After this we strolled round the ancient church with the crooked spire and then had a peek at the town museum. I wish we had not bothered as it spoiled an otherwise perfect visit. If I was being generous I would say that the museum was rather short of things to display. I was hoping that I might find some reference to Philip Stanhope, 4th Earl of Chesterfield, who is reputed to have given his name to the 'Chesterfield' couch, but if it was there I couldn't find it. There were mining artefacts like pit props and clay and tools, but one can only take so many of those. When you get to the section on the town's famous people it gets very thin indeed. The only one of note is George Stephenson, the inventor of the 'Rocket' steam locomotive - and he came from Tyneside, he only died in Chesterfield! I am sorry to sound unappreciative of the efforts of the museum staff here. If it is any encouragement to them I can think of a worse one; it is the Pencil Museum in the Lake District. Why would anyone want to dedicate a museum to pencils?

The only thing that relieves the tedium of Chesterfield Museum is the wonderful Pomegranate Theatre in the basement. The Pomegranate (named after the town's Coat-of-Arms) is the oldest civic theatre in the country and mounts an interesting repertoire of productions over the season in its 546 seat Victorian auditorium. When I noticed a sign saying 'Stage Door' I decided to poke my head inside and have a look. Imagine my shock and horror to find myself on stage, in the middle of a children's pantomime. The stage door led not into a Green room or the wings, but straight onto the proscenium. I stood at the back, halfway through Aladdin, like some enormous, wide-eyed genie, whilst the child actors carried on, oblivious. Fortunately, I managed to retreat before the audience could yell,

"He's behind you!"

Chesterfield to Dore, in Sheffield, is a pleasant drive and if you take a slight detour through Old Whittington, you will find Revolution House. This is a former pub where the Earls of Devonshire and Danby met in 1688, to plan the overthrow of the Catholic James II, in favour of the Protestant William of Orange. It is an interesting little museum, which makes up somewhat for the one in the town centre.

After leaving here you come next to Dronfield and Beauchief (pronounced bee-chief), where there used to be an abbey. There is little evidence of it these days, although its heritage lingers on in the form of 'Abbeydale Brewery'.

The wedding in Dore was that of Simon and Iris. It promised to be a pleasant occasion in several ways, one of which was the chance to catch up with some old friends. Dore is an elegant, leafy place, like much of West Sheffield. It still has a village centre, although it is really now a dormitory suburb. It reminded me that I had enjoyed my years working in Sheffield and I can see why many people come here to work, and then never leave.

Unlike the first wedding this one was not quite in fancy dress, although the groom wore a cowboy hat for most of the proceedings. Simon is always altering his image as part of his grand self-development plan. Despite wearing a cowboy hat his overall appearance was closer to that of 'Swedish Plumber', sporting as he was a 1970s Scandinavian-style moustache. However, this was only the latest in a number of phases he has been through. In his speech, the best man suggested that Simon might like to get himself a selection of Action Man figures, which he could customise to represent his ever-changing image. In addition to Cowboy and Swedish Plumber he could have Jazz Drummer, Fell Runner or French Victorian Gentleman, to name but a few.

One of Simon's self-improvement plans was to learn Spanish, which led him into correspondence with a Mexican girl called Iris. Subsequently, Simon travelled to Mexico to meet Iris in person and now, here we were, celebrating their nuptials in Sheffield. They made a lovely couple, although Simon is well over six feet tall and Iris is under five (I know this because Jane and Iris stood back to back and Iris was the smaller of the two… and Jane is less than five feet tall!).

If for nothing else Dore is famous for being the focus of the first 'wonderland experience' of our trip. Prepare to enter the soft-focus world of myth and legend. You see, Robin Hood came from Dore. 'No!' I hear you protest, 'Robin Hood was from Locksley, probably somewhere near Nottingham'. Well, the thing is, Locksley is a district of Sheffield, just north of Dore, and what's more, Robin Hood had another name, which was Robin Wadsley of Dore. It says so in the Public Records at Kew, where we find a pardon for the famous outlaw for his part in the Peasants' Revolt in York. It reads as follows:

'Robin Hode (Hood) otherwise known as Robin Dore of Wadsley (Yorkshire) given the King's pardon on 22nd May 1382'.

This is not a myth, it is a fact. Consider also that Little John's grave is at nearby Hathersage and that his giant chair sits in a pub there. In addition, if one notes that Peveril Castle, in Castleton, was built by William Peveril the *Sheriff of Nottingham*, then a pattern begins to emerge. The jurisdiction of Nottingham covered this area of Derbyshire but the Yorkshire border was close at hand, and Yorkshire was under the jurisdiction of the Sheriff of York. How easy it would be to poach a few deer in one area and then skip over the border when things got a bit hot. One final proof that Robin Hood was a Yorkshireman is that when he was sick, near the end of his life, he went to Kirklees Abbey in the West Riding to get treatment, which is nowhere near Nottingham! It's the stuff of legend!

Chapter 10
Train to Wonderland

'You may have noticed that I'm not all there myself'
- 'The Cheshire Cat' from 'Alice's Adventures in
Wonderland' - Lewis Carroll

There were times when I managed to catch the train from Sheffield to Manchester. It is a journey that first takes you into Derbyshire and then Cheshire. Perhaps not many people realise that Cheshire, like Staffordshire, strays a little way into the Pennine hills. It is more noted for being completely flat, which is why the radio telescope was sited here, at Jodrell Bank.

Before the train reaches the plains however there are some formidable hills to negotiate, which required some magnificent feats of railway engineering, duly accomplished in the 19th century. The line from Sheffield to Manchester is effectively a branch line, in the sense that it is old-fashioned, slow, cold and rickety. You really wouldn't think that this little two-carriage train was the only railway linking two of the major cities in the country. The problem is the swollen uplands between the two.

Be that as it may, I don't wish to sound curmudgeonly as this line travels through some beautiful scenery and it often appears in lists of the top ten railway journeys in the country or the top fifty railway journeys in the world. I call it 'the train to wonderland'.

You have to be quick to look at the view though because most of the time you are in a tunnel. Two tunnels actually, the Totley Tunnel and the Cowburn Tunnel. These tunnels were excavated between 1888 and 1893, which required an army of men who worked twenty-four hour shifts to meet the deadlines. They were mostly Irish navvies and they were obliged to live in unsanitary conditions, up to thirty of them having to share a house. Things must have been really bad in Ireland for them to consider this a better alternative.

Water kept flooding the workings and accidents were common. At one stage they had to use a diving bell to carry on the work! The workers came to be called 'Moses Men' because every time they struck rocks water spurted out. The combined length of the two tunnels is more than six miles and the Totley Tunnel alone remains the longest un-electrified railway tunnel in the country. No wonder there was only ever one other line traversing this part of the Pennines.

The darkness begins more or less as soon as you leave Sheffield and you don't emerge, blinking into the light, until you get to Grindleford in Derbyshire. It is a funny thing being in a tunnel on a train. You sort of have to prepare a face for your epiphany into the light. Up to that point you can scratch yourself, pick your nose or do whatever you want, as no-one can see you. But as soon as you are illuminated by daylight you have to assume a very British air of nonchalance, diffidence and haughty isolation.

This normally involves staring out of the window, or anything else to avoid having to make eye contact with your fellow passengers. This is fine if there are attractive and interesting things to look at but if you are trailing slowly through some run-down inner city wilderness it becomes a rather tiresome game. It doesn't work at all when they turn lights on in the carriage as you enter a tunnel. All of a sudden you are faced with a stark choice. Either you continue to stare through the window at a sooty wall, or jerk your head forwards and try to find something fascinating in a light fitting or in a piece of half-eaten pizza on the floor.

Near the far end of Totley Tunnel stands a place that will forever live in my memory, for it was here that a modern day Robin Hood charged me more for lunch than it might cost for a short break in Spain – which is in itself a wonder. However, far from approaching it via the bowels of the earth, we were traversing the tops of the hills in 'Auntie', by Stanage Edge. As Hope Valley reveals itself the stern millstone grit gives way to leafy pastures, with playful rivers bumbling their way across the plain below. Although it was Easter there was a late sprinkling of snow covering the hillsides, sparkling under a fierce young sun, which further enhanced the ravishing views.

It was the day after Simon and Iris's wedding and Jane and I were following by road the route of 'the train to wonderland'. It being our twenty-fifth wedding anniversary I had decided to 'bite the bullet' and book a meal at a distinguished hall/restaurant in Derbyshire. You know a place is posh when you can't see it from the road...that is my 'rule of thumb'. Typically, the drive will be so long and tree-lined that it takes several minutes to reach the building. Such was my fate on this day. We parked 'Auntie' as far away from the Bentleys as possible and walked, in our best 'bib and tucker', towards the baronial front door. Before we had reached it, it opened before us and bowing flunkeys ushered us in. Such grace, such refinement you cannot imagine. Our coats were spirited away and we were ingratiated into a lounge of so great a magnificence that it took my breath away. From its hallowed portals I registered mullioned windows, stone inglenooks, leather Chesterfields and acres of lilies.

The waiters were French, and so reverential that with their hushed tones and thick accents it made it practically impossible to know what they were going on about.

We soon found ourselves sipping champagne so I must have agreed to something. It was a bit like enjoying yourself in church - you don't feel quite comfortable.

The menus arrived and after we had got over the embarrassment of whether we would be eating à la carte, or the lowly table d'hôte, we tried to make sense of it. As a potential candidate for an un-reconstituted Northerner I would have you know that I am not a complete philistine. I don't live on pie and peas! Oh yes, I have had my share of oysters and caviar; I know my bouillabaisse from my zarzuela. But this place was out of my league. What is chiboust, or cicely? Is parmesan custard savoury or sweet? Most worryingly, what can you make with pink fir or emulsion that is edible? We were in for a treat.

Thankfully, the staff perceived our dilemma and helpfully guided us through the menu. After we had made our choice we processed through to the elegant dining room, where we were able to engage in witty banter and titter in hushed tones, whilst gazing at the sixty-thousand pound curtains. The meal arrived in a sequence of small but multitudinous parcels, some of them so pretty that I wanted to frame them rather than eat them. Later, when the bill came on a silver salver, it was delivered so deferentially, so professionally, that I felt no pain. It was like a butcher dispatching a sheep. I only had time to blink and open my mouth before the credit card was returned, on the salver, with chocolates and flowers. I won't say how much it cost, that would be crass, but I almost had to be air-lifted to A and E.

Heading home after lunch I noticed how the railway line heads straight through the mountains, whereas on the road we were forced to weave this way and that. The line would disappear for a while, with the only evidence for its existence being the circular towers that were once used as vents for smoke in the days of steam. After Hope the trains fork into Edale Vale, with the road criss-crossing the line at various points.

It is curious to think that in Robin Hood's day, whoever he was, this wonderful, empty landscape was part of the Royal Peak Forest, which stretched from Sherwood, north of Nottingham, right over to Cheshire where we are heading. Of course calling something a forest didn't necessarily mean that the land was covered in trees, it just meant that it was a reserve or hunting area, usually owned by the king.

The western extreme of the old forest is where you can find Lud's Church. It is not really a church but it may have been used for religious rituals in the past. It is a vast fissure in the millstone grit, so deep and narrow that the only time it receives any light is on Midsummer's Day. This is when the pagan rituals are said to have taken place. It is very atmospheric, a wonderland in its own right. It was reputedly a haunt of Robin Hood and Friar Tuck, and it is almost certainly the setting for 'Sir Gawain and the Green

Knight' a 14th century Middle English poem based on an Arthurian legend. In the poem Gawain is challenged by the Green Knight to behead him and if he survives then he would be allowed one return blow. The Green Knight is beheaded but he calmly picks up his own head afterwards. It's a jolly little tale. Tolkien translated it in 1925 and I wonder if he got his ideas for 'The Paths of the Dead' from Lud's Church. More recently, 'Sir Gawain…' has been translated by Yorkshire poet Simon Armitage. I love his account in The Guardian of travelling down to the British Library to read the original manuscript and not being allowed to because he looked too scruffy and spoke too northern. He recounts that the librarian looked at him rather disparagingly and said,

"I'm afraid it doesn't have many pictures in it."

To find Lud's Church you first have to find Gradbach. It is definitely worth a visit if you can locate it but the nearest car park is nearly two miles away and the satnav is not overly helpful.

Whenever we are driving through the Hope Valley Jane likes to pop in to a garden centre just before the turn off to Edale Vale. On this occasion she was looking for some bamboo, which I was not enthusiastic about carrying home in the car. I knew from experience that the bamboo would get everywhere and it would be like travelling in the jungle. Whilst Jane was examining a specimen that wouldn't have looked out of place in Jack and the Beanstalk, I got chatting to a guy who told me that he worked at a small factory nearby. He recounted how one Christmas his workmates had fixed it for him to win a turkey at the annual raffle but that instead of a turkey they had wrapped up three bricks in bubble wrap and Christmas paper, as a joke.

"What happened when you opened it", I wondered?

He chuckled.

"Well," he said, "I wrapped it up again and on my way home I sold it to a bloke at the bus stop."

Soon we were on our way again, peering through the foliage, and forked right into Edale Vale. Edale is where the Pennine Way starts – a long footpath that heads north over Kinder Scout and wends up hill and down dale, only ending on the Scottish borders, at Kirk Yetholm. On any given day you can bump into groups of happy hikers in 'The Nag's Head' in Edale village, getting ready to pursue their own particular wonderland. It appeals to me in principle but on balance I think I would rather drive or take the train.

I don't know whether it was jungle fever brought on by the bamboo but halfway along the vale I noticed a very untypical type of Pennine life lying in the middle of the road, and certainly not one that Robin Hood would have been hunting - it was a wallaby! 'Surely not', I thought to myself and made a mental note to 'take more water with it'. I pulled 'Auntie' over to have a look. It was definitely a wallaby, or a small kangaroo - long face, big ears and enormous feet - and herein lies another little 'wonder' of the peaks. I had heard that there used to be wild wallabies in The Peak District, after some escaped from a private zoo near Leek, in the 1930s, but I had never, ever seen one. Sadly, this one had been knocked down and killed, which is not so unusual because cars are always speeding along this road hitting squirrels, rabbits and other creatures that have not evolved a capacity for road-sense. We couldn't really do anything to help this small antipodean except pull it to the side of the road, where at least it might have a little more dignity in death.

At the western end of Edale Vale lies the second tunnel on the train route from Sheffield, the Cowburn Tunnel. Of course, it cuts straight under the hills whereas 'Auntie' had to struggle to climb the long and winding road above Edale. After another journey in the dark the train emerges at Chinley. If you look left from here you are looking in the direction of a hill called Wormhill. Nothing distinguishes it particularly from any other hill round about – except the name. You see, 'worm' is the Old English word for 'dragon'! Now, many tales are told about dragons in myth and legend. Most countries have them, including the Vikings. In the northeast of the Pennines they tell the tale of the 'Lambton Worm'. It concerns a fisherman, from Lambton, who catches an eel, which turns out to be the devil. He throws it in a well to dispose of it but it grows big by eating the domestic animals of the village and soon becomes a large dragon. It is driven away by the villagers but not very far because it is now so big that it is able to wrap itself around a local hill (Worm Hill) seven times. The dragon begins a reign of terror, demanding tributes and breathing fire but eventually it is killed by a brave knight returning from the Crusades. Does this sound familiar?

The idea of dragons may seem fanciful but recently some researchers have found that the skulls of certain dinosaurs, called hadrosaurs, contain cavities which could have allowed for the storage of naturally produced inflammable chemicals. There are examples of this in the modern natural world. The Bombardier Beetle for example produces hydrogen peroxide and hydroquinone, which it keeps in its body in separate chambers. When approached by a predator it expels these and ignites them, sending out a shooting flame which reaches an intensity of 212 degrees Fahrenheit. So, that accounts for fire-breathing dragons – now, what about flying dragons? Well, one needs look no further than the pterodactyl. I think that proves my case conclusively.

(I must be in a wonderland of my own; like the Cheshire Cat I am sometimes 'not all there!').

Chapter 11
Love Hearts and Wizards

The train to wonderland disembarks at New Mills, just half a mile from the Cheshire border and our trip through wonderland must continue by car. New Mills is that rare thing these days, a Pennine mill-town with a working mill. You might not think of a mill as a likely venue for love but you would be wrong. Cast your mind back to childhood days. Do you remember 'Love Hearts'? They were those colourful, fizzy, circular sweets that we used to eat at Primary School. Well, they are made here in New Mills.

If you are still having trouble remembering what I mean then perhaps the messages will jog your mind. Love Hearts have messages on them. Each and every sweet has on it the outline of a heart, within which is an inscription. What made it wonderland however was the content of the messages. They were the perfect introduction to giggling girls for tongue-tied boys. They would say exciting things like 'I Love You', or 'Kiss Me', outrageous, unspeakable things for boys to utter. What worlds of promise and mystery beckoned when a packet of 'Love Hearts' got shared round.

They are still the same as they were when Swizzels-Matlow started producing them in the 1930s. They began production at a factory in London but moved north for safety reasons during the blitz. They took over an old textile mill in New Mills and have remained there ever since. Thank goodness they have resisted the temptation to modernise the messages to such things as 'Let's have it off', or 'Get Stuffed'.

You pass Swizzells factory on the way back from Sheffield to Manchester, and now we come to Cheshire. We are still heading west, to the very extremities of the Pennines, which have a last fling at Alderley Edge before fizzling out on the Cheshire Plain. As soon as you cross the border into Cheshire the number plates on the cars become ten years younger. If you have a registration older than one year then you are looked down upon. Everyone travels round in those great, four-wheel drive obsidian blocks, which look as if they have been chiselled out of basalt from Fingal's Cave. They are normally to be spotted on the school run, or with their engine running parked outside shops. However, when in 'Auntie', I drive fearlessly towards them, not cowed by their bullying appearance.

I exaggerate of course but there is an element of truth here. Cheshire is, by and large, a wealthy county. A few years ago Victoria Wines confirmed that their branch in Alderley Edge sold more champagne than any other branch in the country. Of course this is Footballers Wives territory, home to David Beckham and so on but there is also a lot of old money here. In the nineteenth century Alderley Edge was called Chorley, which means 'peasants clearing'. This probably wasn't acceptable to the city traders and cotton barons, who had settled there with the advent of the railway, and so they changed the name.

On the way to Alderley Edge we called in at my own personal wonderland, 'The Swan Inn' at Kettleshulme, with the flag of St George flying proudly above it (remember the dragons). If you want to experience a real country inn, which is an increasingly rare thing, then you will find a gem here.

The Swan has been trading as a public house for the best part of five hundred years, as far as anyone can tell – the deeds have been lost in the mists of time. It is quite likely because The Swan stands on the old 'salt route', the pack-horse trail from the salt-mines of South Cheshire, across the Pennines to Sheffield and beyond. You get lots of old inns along this road, some of them even older than The Swan, and some sadly fallen into disuse.

To me The Swan is 'Paradise Regained' but it was nearly 'Paradise Lost' several years ago when the owner at that time decided to turn it from a pub into his own home. Several of us thought that this would be a tragedy and made a co-operative effort to buy it off him. Eventually we succeeded and, with a letter from Prince Charles endorsing the project, The Swan was re-born. This co-operative model has become quite a popular way to save endangered pubs and I must say it was a great experience for me. The pub was rescued, for the time being at least and after a few years we found a new buyer who was prepared to keep it and cherish it.

Why bother saving it you may ask? Well, I think that there is something unique about the village inn. John Betjeman wrote –

'The village inn, the good, old inn,
So ancient, clean and free from sin'.

This is all very true in the case of The Swan. You could bring your old mother here, or your children, and they would not be scandalized by improper behaviour. On the contrary they would be made to feel most welcome. There is good conversation and banter to listen to (or to join in) and you feel involved because the whole place is cosy and intimate. There is a roaring fire in winter - beams, settles, good beer and good food. What more could you want?

Today, as usual, there was some witty repartee flying around. I had changed out of my suit since lunch and happened to be wearing a T-shirt and gilet, with shorts and trainers (not the epitome of fashion I admit, but perfectly serviceable). When he saw me, one of the farmers at the bar snorted and said,

"Did you walk through a washing line on your way in?"

That is the sort of thing I have to put with at The Swan.

The road takes a pretty wild roller-coaster ride from Kettleshulme, through Pott Shrigley and Bollington, before gradually descending into Prestbury and Alderley Edge.

It is remarkable how this large dormitory village keeps bucking the trend of economic recession. It is the most expensive area in the country after Chelsea and Kensington and if you go onto a property website you have to scroll through more than twenty pages if you want something for less than seven figures. Houses for sale at £20M are not unknown.

From time to time when I was eighteen, my friend and I used to frequent the pubs of Alderley Edge. We didn't have much money so, to impress the girls, we would carry Rolls Royce and Aston Martin key-fobs and display them ostentatiously. If any girls had ever agreed to go out with us they would have been sadly disappointed when they got to the car park. This heady atmosphere of youth and money is a type of wonderland I suppose but we have come here for an altogether darker purpose – the wizard!

'The Edge' part of Alderley Edge is a sandstone outcrop, sticking up from the Cheshire plain. It connects to the westerly slopes of the Pennines and so it is acceptable that we include it in our journey. It is a heavily wooded hill with a north facing crag, from where you can overlook Manchester and the Cheshire Plain. Just to the west of the crag face there is a path which descends into the woods. You have to keep your wits about you because the Edge is full of little paths that cross this way and that, through some dense and remarkably similar woodland. The trees are all twisted, knotted and fallen and there are sudden drops to avoid. It is very easy to get lost here, especially in the dark, but you wouldn't want to visit in the dark, for reasons that I shall explain.

I used to know the Edge pretty well when I was a youth but I hadn't been there for many years and Jane hadn't been at all. I wanted to show off my local knowledge and so, eschewing guidebooks and their ilk, I ushered my better half and Meg down the path and into the covering woods. I don't know if you are familiar with the works of Alan Garner. He is a local writer, mainly of children's fantasy, and he has based a lot of his work on the stories that surround the Edge, particularly 'The Weirdstone of Brisingamen', which is set exclusively around this area. It concerns the use of magic and secret magical armies that slumber inside the Edge. The Edge is indeed riddled with caves and mines. The Romans mined lead here and copper has been mined from the Bronze Age onwards. Many of the entrances are completely open and can be accessed (although they should not be!).

I was keen to share the delights of this mysterious place and persuaded Jane that we could have a peek at the mines. Jane was doubtful but the poor dear trusts me and the dog was on a lead and couldn't argue, so we headed for one of the many scar-like entrances. I pointed out the copper seams and the ancient graffiti on the walls – evidence of Man's connection with the Edge, which dates back to pre-history. Outside the copper mine stands the Golden Stone, which is probably an ancient Standing Stone, designed to mark and protect it. There is evidence of earthen circles and also a stone Druids Circle. At various times of year Pagans, Druids and those of the Wicca Way still meet there. I always thought that the Wicca Way was an aisle at IKEA but, apparently, it is a type of religion.

We entered the mine and at first all went well; however, as we pressed further in the roof started to get lower. This didn't affect Jane so much, as she is only small, but I had to stoop. I thought I knew these caves well, I really did, but after I had tripped over the same lump of sandstone twice I started to get worried. I don't know how long we wandered around but I kept up a witty banter until, eventually, I noticed a grey light appearing in front of us, which soon announced itself as the entrance we had taken some time ago. Jane never suspected a thing.

I was relieved but our troubles weren't over yet, as it was rapidly going dark outside and a mist was beginning to swirl amongst the twisted trees. This gave them a rather threatening appearance and so we set a brisk pace back to the car. Unfortunately, all the paths on the Edge look the same and we made little progress.

We kept forking off and then having to double back because I was looking for a landmark, like the Armada Beacon, which perches on top of an even older structure - a burial chamber or 'barrow'. Everywhere looked the same and both Jane and Meg began to be worried. Meg is a real coward in such situations and will happily walk off with a stranger if they seem to be taking a better path. Jane was just telling me to fork off again (at least I think it was 'fork') when we stumbled upon the Wizard's Well. This was something I recognised at last and I breathed a sigh of relief. The Wizard's Well is underneath a rock face on which there is an interesting engraving and inscription. There is a little spring coming out of the rock which falls into a stone trough on the ground, and above the trough are an inscription and a carving of the face of an old man with a beard. The inscription says:

'Drink this water, take thy fill,
For the water falls by the Wizard's will'.

They say that the water never dries up, even in a drought. There is a pub nearby called 'The Wizard' and it was here, the story goes, that one dark and misty morning a farmer, on the way to market to sell his white mare, met an old man with a long beard, wearing a cloak and carrying a staff. The old man wanted to buy the mare but the farmer refused, hoping for a better price at Macclesfield market. The old man told him that he would not be able to sell the mare at market and then he vanished into the mist. Duly, the farmer couldn't sell his mare and on the way home he bumped into the old man again, at the same spot, who again offered to buy the horse. This time the farmer agreed and the old man then revealed himself to be a wizard. He took the farmer and his horse into the caves on the Edge where he was shown an army of sleeping knights, each with a white horse, except for one. The wizard explained that the farmer's horse would make up the numbers so to speak and that the slumbering army would arise and fight for England in her darkest hour.

It felt like *our* darkest hour had just passed, but we hadn't encountered any knights who might have helped us! This story was popularised by the vicar of Nether Alderley in a sermon in 1753, and it brings us to our last wonderland, because that also originates with a clergyman, from not far away. The clergyman is Charles Dodgson, better known as Lewis Carroll, and the wonderland is, as you probably know, one that began with Alice.

I really liked 'Alice in Wonderland' as a child – all those weird, fantastical creatures, and the stereotypes and caricatures of Victorian society. I loved the humour and the magic and found the book in no way threatening or disturbing, as some people do apparently.

Lewis Carroll was born in Daresbury, Cheshire, just a hop, skip and a jump to the west of Alderley Edge. Carroll's father was curate of All Saints parish church in Daresbury, and the family lived here until Lewis was eleven years old, when his father was appointed as priest to a church in Croft-on-Tees, in North Yorkshire. Daresbury is a pretty little village, built using the warm red sandstone so prevalent in Cheshire. The church is no exception to this and is worth investigation in its own right, despite the Carroll connection. Some of the stained glass depicts characters and scenes from 'Alice in Wonderland'. Obviously, they have been installed since the publication of the story but on the outside of the building there are some ancient carvings of animals, one of which is definitely a grinning cat!

There has been some debate recently about whether Lewis Carroll had an unhealthy interest in young girls. There is little doubt that the Alice of the story is based on Alice Liddell, the young daughter of a family friend. Carroll's diaries do suggest a man tormented by inner demons and keenly aware of his own failings, but I don't want to think of him for these reasons. I would rather remember the story and the enjoyment it gives me. The knowledge that he had brought pleasure to people through his writing would have pleased Carroll I think. I particularly like the following quote from him:

"I have reason to believe that Alice has been read by some hundreds of English children aged from five – fifteen; also by children aged from fifteen – twenty-five; yet again by children aged from twenty-five – thirty-five, and even children – for there are such- in whom no waning of health or strength, no weariness of the solemn mockery and the gaudy glitter, and the hopeless misery of life has availed to parch the pure fountain of joy that wells up in all child-like hearts!"

I wish you could put that on a Love Heart.

Chapter 12
The Un-reconstituted North

'The only place in England which escapes our characteristic
vice of snobbery'
- AJP Taylor (on Manchester)

From time to time I am accused of being an 'un-reconstituted northerner'. What do they mean? Is it my manners? Do I scratch myself in public or pass wind at inappropriate moments? Perhaps it's my Nordic vowel sounds. In my case it probably refers to a predisposition to make for the pub at the earliest opportunity. I might be un-reconstituted in this sense but consider this - is it such a good thing to be merely *'reconstituted'*? Not, I suggest, if I were meat!

Anyway, if we are all un-reconstituted then why is there so much interest in the North? I cannot turn on the TV these days, without seeing programmes on sheep-shearing in the Lake District or how to make Wensleydale Cheese - plus any number of shows about antiques, set in Yorkshire. Is it because there is something true, honest and 'gritty' in the northern character that attracts people, or is it just a fascination for observing the natives in their natural habitat? Most likely it is the appeal of returning to some quieter, less complicated existence, amongst beautiful surroundings; following some instinct to 'get away from it all' or to 'find ourselves'.

The Northern hills may be popular but there is still prejudice about the towns and cities of the North, and about northerners in general. I listened to a comedian on the radio some time ago and he was making jokes about 'grotty' places 'Up North'. For example, he thought it was funny to call Greater Manchester, 'Crater Manchester', the implication being that it would be better if some nuclear holocaust were to remove the city entirely. After demolishing Manchester he moved on to Hull, which had suffered a lot of damage to the city centre in the floods of 2007.

"How much would that cost to repair?" he quipped, wittily, "£12.50!?"

Hilarious! I am not going to deny that there are some run-down places in Manchester, but that applies to towns everywhere doesn't it? Wasn't it John Betjeman who wished for Slough to be destroyed by German bombs?

In the year 2000 there was a bid for the Olympics to be staged in Manchester. When the day came for the results to be announced people gathered in front of a big screen at Castlefields, an open-air venue not far from Manchester city centre and the site of an old Roman fort. There wasn't a massive amount of excitement despite the media's best attempts to manufacture it and when the rejection of the bid was announced it was accepted with resignation and a certain quiet dignity. You couldn't escape the impression that there had been only lukewarm support for Manchester from the country at large, even from some British athletes, who openly came out in favour of Sydney's bid.

Some cited the weather as a problem. When I pointed out to friends of mine that the August rainfall in Sydney was greater than that of Manchester, the huffy response was that they would rather have rainstorms in Sydney than perpetual drizzle in Manchester. You can understand why the Mancunians seemed a bit crestfallen.

Part of the problem is that the South simply won't allow the North to develop. As a nation we are so London-centric. Of course London is a great city but it gets *so* much. For example, as I write there has been news about the latest investments in transport infrastructure in the UK. In London the amount is £3,000 per capita, but in parts of the North the figure is as low as £5 per capita!

Certainly there have been 'enterprise zones' in the north but often businesses are quietly moved south when the government money runs out. How many people remember that 'The Guardian' newspaper was originally 'The Manchester Guardian'? It became so successful that it simply *had* to move to London. It is as if there is a gravitational force put out by the Southeast, which will eventually end up as one giant car park cum airport.

To make up for losing the Olympics, Manchester was awarded the Commonwealth Games in 2002, as a sort of consolation prize. Money was invested in a new stadium in the east of the city along with a velodrome and other facilities and this was a creditable attempt to regenerate areas in decline, like Middleton, Gorton and Harper Hey.

Outside the stadium, which is now home to Manchester City F.C., an excellent sculpture was erected in steel, called 'B of the Bang'. It was named after the athlete Linford Christie, who famously stated that he liked to be away so quickly off the starting-blocks that it would be on the 'B' of the bang of the starting-pistol. The installation was huge and of imaginative design, representing the explosion from a discharging gun. It was like a copper-coloured firework with lots of sharp points at the top. From the outset it had structural problems and bits of the 'bang', in the form of shards weighing several hundred-weight, kept falling off and slicing into the ground. It became lethal, and had to be taken down, which was a pity because sculptures do have a way of creating atmosphere, character and identity.

As a family we don't go to many sporting events but the Commonwealth Games brought an infectious excitement and pride to Manchester and we decided to attend the closing ceremony, partly because the Queen was going to be there and we had never seen her before. All went well and schoolchildren performed various dances with torches, as is common with such events, but actually we would probably have had a better view on the TV. I asked an official if we could move forward a bit and we were given seats amongst the South African team.

A wave of excitement travelled around the stadium as the Queen and her Consort arrived and we all felt the eyes of many millions of people focused on Manchester.

Up to that point Manchester had avoided living up to its reputation for rain. There had been a little during the week but mostly it had been sunny. The closing ceremony continued happily up to the point where the official handover was to take place, to the mayor of the next city to host the Games, Melbourne.

In retrospect it might have been a good idea to provide a covered platform or canopy for the main speakers. As soon as the Mayor of Melbourne started to speak, thanking his hosts and so on, there was a complete and utter cloudburst; the heavens opened - wide! The rain started to bounce off the head and shoulders of the poor man as he manfully carried on with his speech. I mean, nobody even had an umbrella! If the microphones had short-circuited the entire party of dignitaries could have been electrocuted. As for his very expensive-looking suit - well - and all this was visible in high definition, on giant screens situated at strategic points round the stadium, as well as being beamed halfway round the world.

Meanwhile I was having a minor personal crisis. On the way in we had bought some cheap, transparent plastic rain capes. Now it was pouring down and we were very glad of them. Absorbed as I was in the farce taking place below I didn't notice the water starting to collect in my plastic-covered lap. The seats were smallish and my knees were squeezed in at an acute angle, which meant that when I did finally notice it quite a large pool had developed. The question was what to do with it. Whichever way that I tipped it I was going to soak a South African athlete. Specifically, if I went to the side I would soak someone's knees, and if I emptied it forwards I would soak someone's head. The situation was reaching crisis point and I decided that the only solution was to tip the water backwards towards my stomach and then I could lean down and try to suck it up. Frustratingly, it was difficult to regulate the flow of water into my mouth and it poured all over my face and everywhere else. Panicking I tried to swallow as much of the wretched stuff as I could with the result that I began to choke. I coughed, wheezed and retched. The water went everywhere and the attention of South African athletics was briefly turned away from the Queen and on to me. They regarded me with astonishment as I leapt out of my seat and waded through them down towards the exit, making strange, inarticulate gargling noises, like some lunatic or anarchist bent on mischief. By the time I had got through them all they were probably short of a sprinter or two.

Normally, I would be watching Manchester from high up a hill, in Lyme Park, and it is at this point that I must declare an interlude in our travels. You see, Jane and I live on the southern edges of Manchester, just on the borders of the Peak District and, however hard I might try, I cannot pretend to visit the city as a tourist – I know it too well. So, like the chapter on Sheffield, the ones on Manchester are going to be a bit of a retrospective. I hope you enjoy them.

The Pennines surround Manchester on three sides, like the rim of a bowl. Manchester nestles into the hills, comfortable and protected, like a nursing infant. Indeed the original name for Manchester was Mamucium, 'mam' being a Celtic word for 'female breast' (where also we get 'mam' or 'mum' for mother).

Lyme Hall is 'Pemberley', where Mr Darcy took Elizabeth Bennett to live in the 1995 BBC production of 'Pride and Prejudice', and from there you can watch the sunset over town and the lights beginning to twinkle. I never tire of the routine, dog at side, as we roam about this enormous deer park, and observe the grand scale of the city gradually unfold before us (however I rarely do a 'Colin Firth' and dive into a pond).

With a population of almost three million people Greater Manchester is much bigger than Sheffield, Leeds, Liverpool, Glasgow and Bristol and it is the about the same size as Birmingham. A survey in The New York Times recently ranked Manchester at no. 20 in the world for cities worth visiting, ahead of Singapore, Dresden and Miami. London came in at no. 7 but I still think that Manchester's achievement is remarkable.

As I look down from my vantage point I can make out city landmarks, such as Manchester University, where the atom was first split, and where the first programmable computer was created. I can see the Bridgewater Hall, home to the world famous Halle orchestra, and the outline of the John Rylands Library, guardian of the earliest fragments of John's Gospel.

At a more prosaic level there is the Midland Hotel, where Mr Rolls first met Mr Royce and just to the left of it Old Trafford, the 'Theatre of Dreams'. There are the bright lights of Spinningfields, the new financial district and, tallest and most recent addition, the iconic Beetham Tower.

There are many features to pick out if you have an experienced eye, such as the Lowry Centre and Media City in Salford or, the slightly oppressive, Imperial War Museum North. Scan further west and you notice The Trafford Centre, with its great central dome, like Mammon's answer to St. Mark's Basilica. Scan east, past the snaking lights of the 'curry-mile' and there is the Town Hall which has, as I am sure the mayor would tell you, more bricks in it than the Houses of Parliament. Finally, you see the cathedral, the National Football Museum, the C.I.S. building, and Eastlands, home to Manchester City.

Looking at the two football stadia together, United in the West and City in the East I am reminded of how these world-famous football clubs started. United began in 1878 as an amateur team, formed by a branch of the Lancashire and Yorkshire Railway. They were based at Newton Heath in the northeast of Manchester and subsequently nicknamed 'The Heathens'. Whether United's modern nickname of 'The Red Devils' came from this is debatable. Perhaps it was because, unlike City, they were not affiliated to a church. Manchester City was founded by St Mary's Roman Catholic Church in Gorton in 1880. Many modern Football League clubs were formed by the Church in Victorian times as a means of giving the working man something to do, to stop him getting into trouble. Unfortunately, trouble followed when different branches of the Christian Church founded clubs near to each other. Protestant teams and Catholic teams took tribal positions and healthy rivalry slipped into something darker. Thankfully, these days this religious aspect of club rivalry is not quite so extreme in Manchester, arguably unlike other cities, such as Liverpool or Glasgow.

Manchester United has become one of the most popular football clubs in the world, with an estimated 330 million supporters globally, and Manchester City is not far behind. Since being bought by Sheikh Monsour of The United Arab Emirates in 2008, Eastlands has inevitably been nicknamed 'Middle East-lands'.

Have I made the case for Manchester yet? I suppose you want some amusing anecdotes involving sex and violence? Well, alright – if you insist!

I was a relatively young man when I met a girl from London and started going out with her. She came to visit me in Manchester and I wanted to impress her with the things that the city had to offer. I gathered that she had been well brought up and had had quite a sheltered childhood - to date. Her father was in the diplomatic service and worked for the British Council in Karachi. If you have read my prologue then you will have met her already.

I had heard of a characterful pub called 'Tommy Duck's', but I had never been. It was near the Palace Theatre where we were going later to take in a show, so it seemed the perfect venue for a lunch-time sojourn. I swaggered into Tommy Duck's with my pretty, petite, shy girlfriend, trying to appear sophisticated. What we got was characterful alright, but not quite in the way I had expected. For the first and only time in my life I found myself in a pub with a topless barmaid!

I did not dare to look at my girlfriend, still less the barmaid, and I ushered her into a side room out of the way. Here my horror only increased because every available bit of wall space in the room, including the ceiling, had women's knickers nailed to it! Shocked, we dashed back out onto the street and I tried to make light of it, but that was probably the point where our relationship began to go downhill.

Well, that deals with sex. For the violence you will have to meet my friend, Brian.

Chapter 13
Take This and That

'Manchester's not missing anything except a beach'
- attributed to Ian Brown, 'The Stone Roses'

Do you want to know one of the best little curry houses in Manchester? It is called 'This and That' and it is on Soap Street, just on the edge of the Northern Quarter. Soap Street is not easy to find but when you do - what a treat awaits! It looks like a scene from a 1930s gangster movie, set in Chicago. It is a mean, narrow alley complete with grimy warehouses, cast-iron fire escapes and leaky gutters that drip, disconsolately, into oily puddles. At any moment you expect a stranger to step out of a dark corner, wearing a gabardine and Homburg hat, to ask you for a light. Apparently, scenes from the film 'Chicago' were shot here because it has the authentic 1930s Chicago 'feel' that Chicago itself no longer possesses.

It was Brian who first took me to 'This and That', but Brian doesn't really notice things like surroundings, because he is blind. I was accompanying him and his daughter to a small reception at the Town Hall, in recognition of his work for charity. Brian had cycled round the British Isles on the back of a tandem to raise money for Well Spring, a charity for the homeless. First though it was time for food, and 'This and That' had been Brian's choice. There were just the two of us because his daughter had refused to walk down Soap Street! Outside the 'restaurant' was a large wheelie-bin (from behind which an assassin might jump at any moment!) and stuck to the window was a board with the menu on it. 'This and That' is famous for its 'Rice and Three', which consists of three curries and a portion of rice. This will set you back the princely sum of £4. The place might have looked off-putting but, with Yorkshire blood in my veins, I was lured in because it was so cheap!

I wouldn't say the interior was sumptuous but it was clean. There were plastic chairs, Formica-topped tables and a vinyl floor. In fact, it reminded me of a 1950s 'Milk Bar'. As soon as the staff saw Brian they greeted him warmly and engaged him in friendly conversation. He was obviously well known here. This is one of the great blessings about an excursion with Brian - he brings out the best in people. He is so positive about life despite his disability, although he is constantly getting into scrapes. For example, he loves playing football; you simply have to point him in the right direction for goal. He would probably even have a go at driving a car if anyone were mad enough to let him.

All the cooking at 'This and That' is done in front of you and the dishes of the day are displayed in a bain-marie. You can help yourself to whatever you fancy and at the same time chat with the chef about the fortunes of Manchester City. The curry was delicious and when I went back for a samosa and an onion bhaji they gave me second helpings! Don't imagine that the place is the Indian equivalent of a 'greasy spoon café' – there were professional people eating here as well as locals. The only worrying part of the whole proceedings was visiting the loo where, in authentic Asian style, they had only a pot of water. Loo rolls were available on request! I said to Brian that if I was not ill the next morning I would definitely come again. I was fine next day and have returned subsequently many times.

This area of Manchester is one of the oldest parts of the city but also one of the trendiest, with street art by Banksy on the walls and members of famous bands hanging round the bars. I tend to avoid shops like the plague but my wife and daughter inform me that the shopping is good hereabouts. A good excuse to shun the shops was the fact that I was with Brian, because my shopping experiences with him have not always ended successfully. There was the time we went to a

DIY store and I steered Brian round to prevent him injuring people with the 9ft length of skirting board he was carrying. A kind shop assistant helped us out to the car park with this piece of two by four, but it was immediately obvious to me that it was not going to fit into the car.

"Yes it will," Brian tried to reassure me.

"No it won't, honestly," I replied.

"Not even diagonally?"

"No."

"No," agreed the shop assistant.

"Let's just give it a try," said Brian, ever the optimist. There was nothing else for it.

"Alright," I agreed reluctantly.

We tried putting the wretched plank in at every conceivable angle, with Brian pulling at the front and me and the shop-assistant pushing at the back. After a long struggle we eventually managed it by resting one end on the dashboard and then placing it, as Brian had suggested, diagonally, so that the other end was in the boot compartment. Phew! All we had to do now was close the boot lid.

Wasn't it Archimedes who said that if you gave him a big enough lever he could move the world? The boot wouldn't close at first because the board was in the way. We jiggled it this way and that but it was becoming increasingly clear that whilst the wood was

9ft long, the car was only 8ft 6 inches. Eventually, losing patience with the boot, the board, Brian and the world, I gave the thing a final shove and slammed shut the boot. Unfortunately, the lid caught the skirting with considerable force and sent it flying forward. It hit the dashboard, bent momentarily and then, with an almighty crash, went straight through the windscreen, ending up hanging halfway down the bonnet. It was a perfect demonstration of Archimedes principle.

"What's happening Pete?" asked Brian.

"I wish I knew," I replied, feeling pretty peeved with my friend. I didn't think that Brian was bringing out the best in me on this occasion.

Does that deal with violence? It is the most I have ever seen in Manchester.

I forgave Brian after a little while. You can't stay mad with him for long. How can you fault a bloke who goes cycling round the country on the back of a tandem to raise money for charity; or who is happy to cut the top of your enormous conifer hedge, perched atop a ladder; or who cheerfully crawls around your drain to unblock it, and who even buys you the occasional drink?

To get Brian to buy me a drink was my next object after leaving 'This and That'. However, I will avoid the temptation to start talking about pubs again and describe as best as I am able the culture to be had around Cathedral Square, which is a short walk from Soap Street. I must say though that the 'Marble Arch' pub is a wonder of Victorian architecture, with a fabulously tiled interior. It is home to 'Marble Brewery' a 'micro' that sprang up in the shadow of the old Boddingtons Brewery, now sadly defunct.

Anyway, we had a beer there and then wandered over to the Cathedral Gardens, past the 'MEN Arena' - where 'Take That' were due to perform; past the National Football Museum, to Chetham's Library.

Chetham's Music School library is the oldest public lending library in the UK, opening as it did in 1653. It is the legacy of Humphrey Chetham, a prominent textile merchant, banker and landowner who took over the former monastery and turned it into a school for the poor, of which the library was only part. These days it is a music school but you can still visit the magnificent sandstone Tudor buildings and sit where Marx and Engels met in the 19th century to talk and write about the poor working conditions in the Manchester cotton industry. Apparently Chinese tourists come here as a kind of pilgrimage and weep as they stand in the place where the philosophy of Communism was first mooted.

Perhaps you are thinking that all this is not much use to Brian, but he really appreciates things if you take the trouble to describe them for him; a bit of moss on a wall, an engraving, the cover of an old book.

After leaving Chetham's Brian and I wandered off to the Town Hall for Brian's reception. We trekked west, past the cathedral and the Manchester Eye; past Sinclair's Oyster Bar, the Shambles and the Hanging

Ditch; past Harvey Nichols, Selfridges and all those purveyors of 'tissued fripperies' - to St Ann's Square and the Royal Exchange building. Built as a trading hall for Manchester's Cotton Exchange, The Royal Exchange building now houses a magnificent theatre, perhaps my favourite theatre space in the world. The original interior has been retained, with the figures for the last day of trading still visible on boards high up on the walls, below a mighty domed ceiling. The enormous floor of the Exchange has also been retained, with boutiques, galleries, bars and restaurants now adorning the side. The whole place resonates with Victorian elegance, except for one thing; in the centre of the floor an alien spacecraft has landed!

It squats spider-like... a giant pod with four tubular steel legs, which thrust into the enormous stone pillars that support the great dome. It screams for your attention this steel and glass extravagance, this building within a building. You might think that it would clash with its surroundings but the effect is just to thrill, as two eras are forced to live together. It is not a space ship though - it is the Royal Exchange Theatre, which has been the scene of some terrific productions since its inception in 1976. Just about anybody who is anybody has played here, including the great Michael Hordern. I remember him putting in a brilliant performance in the rather strange play, 'The Ordeal of Gilbert Pinfold'. For some scenes they actually flooded the stage and floated boats on it, which was quite a feat.

What I like so much about the theatre is that although it holds 700 people it remains an intimate space because it is in the round, with the front row (or 'banquettes' as they are known) only inches away from the actors, who occasionally end up landing on members of the audience. The banquettes are cheap seats (nine pounds in 2011), but I always think that their name (pronounced 'bonk-ettes') sounds like some Motown backing group.

Just across the way from the theatre is St. Ann's Church, the second church of Manchester after the cathedral. It is a Grade I listed building designed in the 18th century by John Barker, the pupil of Christopher Wren, and lends its name to the square on which it stands. Next to the church is 'Mr Thomas's Famous Chop House', a Manchester landmark since Victorian times, where I noticed a really clever bit of graffiti scrawled on the wall of the 'Gents':

'Karl Marx: to be is to do.
Jean-Paul Sartre: to do is to be.
Frank Sinatra: do-be-do-be-do'.

Brian disgraced himself by mistakenly walking into the 'Ladies'. A lot of screaming ensued but Brian was unrepentant.

Just along the road from Tom's Chop House is Albert Square, where you will find the Town Hall, and the Central Library to one side of it. Central Library is a large, circular building made of stone, and another fine Victorian-style edifice. I like it mostly for the top floor, which contains thousands of books on bookshelves that fan out like the spokes of a wheel. You will find many studious people poring over books at any one time and I always get a rise from coughing or by shutting a book a little too loudly, prompting frowning faces to look up as the echo travels around the room (I have a feeling that I also mentioned this with reference to the Buxton campus of The University of Derby. I really ought to grow up).

Nearby is the 'Church of the Hidden Gem', so called because it looks to be just part of an ordinary-looking terrace of buildings; however, when you go inside you find a most attractive Catholic church, which is lit by hundreds of candles. It always features a display of interesting artwork, viewed by a steady and ever-changing stream of worshippers. You have to look hard to find this place but just remember it by the street it is located on, the unusually named Brazennose Street.

Also of note round this part of town is Lincoln Square where there is a statue of that great American president. It was presented to Manchester by the United States Government at the end of the American Civil War, in 1865, because of the city's refusal to buy cotton from the rebellious Confederacy.

If you want to play a good game you can walk along a series of covered passages or 'ginnels' all the way from St Ann's Square to Lincoln Square and beyond. To go further though you have to walk through the front door of a pub and then out of the back door into the next street. You go up St Ann's Passage, then up

Boardmen's Entry, before emerging in Brazennose Street and Tasle Alley (I swear I am not taking these names from a 'Carry On' film).

Like many northern cities Manchester boasts an impressive town hall. It is built of hard sandstone in the neo-gothic style and the grand clock tower soars to 285 feet, just 31 feet short of Big Ben. It houses twenty-three bells, the biggest of which is Great Abel, who marks the hours over Albert Square and St Peter's Square. We were led into the Great Hall, via the sweeping staircase that bears the symbol of Manchester on its steps - a 'busy bee'. The Great Hall has an interesting and impressive set of murals depicting the history of Manchester, painted in 1879 by Ford Madox Brown. A particular mural caught my eye, which hinted at some Viking connection with the city. It was entitled 'The Expulsion of the Danes from Manchester' and depicted a crowd of angry Mancunians beating some prostrate Vikings with clubs. The Vikings sailed up the Mersey to conquer Manchester, but were repulsed. They have been doing that to Liverpudlians ever since!

Looking at murals was not really Brian's thing and he wandered off to examine the classical statuary of the grand hall, by touch. As chance would have it, he was just running his fingers over the bust of some particularly well-endowed, marble nymph, when in walked the mayoral party. It was an embarrassing moment. Brian tried to explain that things were not as they seemed but the edge had gone off the occasion somehow!

After the ceremony we headed out of the Town Hall, into St Peter's Square, with the vague aim of finding the spot where the Vikings were repulsed.

When I watched a recent Panorama programme on 'The Manchester Riots' of 2011, I was tempted to say 'nothing changes', but this would be a travesty of the truth. It wasn't really the Manchester riots, as far as I could tell, but the *London* riots that Panorama should have concentrated on. They started it! The main thing that irritated me about the riots in Manchester was the graffiti that was scrawled on the fascinating sculpture which stands outside the Bridgewater Hall. The sculpture is by Japanese sculptor Kan Yasuda and it takes the form of a giant pebble made out of Carrara marble. It is called 'Touchstone' and its smooth texture invites you to run your fingers over the surface. What it doesn't invite you to do is spray-paint it, which was what one disgruntled youth had done.

Bridgewater Hall lies next to the Bridgewater Canal and behind the Midland Hotel, which is itself opposite the Town Hall. It was built as the new home for the Halle Orchestra and the BBC Philharmonic Orchestra, after the Free Trade Hall was turned into a hotel in the 1990s. On the other side of the hall from the canal is a tramway where heavy trams rumble along a viaduct all day. This did not bode well for recording the BBC Phil because of the vibration, and so the architects of the new Bridgewater hit upon a cunning plan - they decided to build the entire building on springs! This means that the whole place is really a floating island.

I was privileged to be one of the first to get a tour round the building when it opened, in 1996. There is a narrow rubber skirt around the perimeter, which marks the boundary of the 'island'. When you step over this you land in the atrium of the concert hall. Once inside the first thing you notice are some shiny brass double doors leading into the auditorium. They are not supposed to be shiny; they are designed to build up an interesting patina of fingerprints from the thousands of visitors and employees who travel through them. I suppose it is a nod in the direction of Yasuda's Touchstone outside. Sadly, the day I visited some over enthusiastic cleaner had decided to really tackle those dull doors and had given them a good polish with 'Brasso'. They shone spectacularly!

Our party was shown the auditorium and galleries and then finally we were led underground to the basement, to see the springs. Frankly, this was quite scary when you realise that nearly 26,000 tons of building is looming above you and only prevented from falling and squashing you by some steel springs. This was the first time such technology had been used but, anyway, the place is still standing. I contemplated what might happen if all the concert-goers started to jump up and down at the same time. Would the building begin to bounce up and down and then take off along Deansgate like some enormous pogo stick?

The Vikings must have been expelled from somewhere round here because this is the area of Manchester that was first inhabited, and the site of the Roman fort of Mamucium. The Vikings would sail up the River Mersey, pillaging and plundering, but were turned back by Saxons, like Aethelfleda, warrior daughter of King Alfred. Just to the west of here the modern towns of Widnes and Runcorn were particularly bloody areas of battle, a fact remembered these days in the naming of the Widnes rugby league team as 'The Widnes Vikings'. It seems like the Mersey acted as a bit of a frontier, constantly being fought over by the Vikings and the Anglo-Saxons. You can see the area these days by taking a boat trip up the Manchester Ship Canal to Salford Quays. Better still you can read all about it in a book called 'Shadowers Crossing', by Chris Kirwan.

I had a little task of my own to undertake whilst I was in this part of town, which took Brian and I to Manchester Art Gallery. I had a painting I wanted valuing – one that I had inherited from my parents some years before - and I was keen to find out what it was worth. I discovered that the art gallery did valuations every Wednesday afternoon and so it was that Brian and I found ourselves stepping over the threshold of this 'cathedral' of high culture.

I was a tad overawed by the magnificent portico and entered its portals tentatively, clutching my picture in sweaty hands. The lady on reception looked at us searchingly and directed us to a small room at the side.

Inside it was like a doctor's surgery, with several people sitting around holding works of art. The 'patients' looked up expectantly as we walked in but immediately sank back into their chairs again. The receptionist smiled efficiently,

"The art historian will see you soon" she said, and turning clipped importantly out of the room.

I looked doubtfully at my piece of 'art'. It didn't look very impressive next to some of the pieces belonging to the others. It was a painting of a river beside a wood, with a mountain in the background. I can see now that it was really a pretty crude daub. The river looked like it was frozen, the trees were stiff and stick-like and they appeared to float above the river somehow. In the foreground was a sheep, which seemed as if it might be suffering from terminal constipation. As for the mountain – it most resembled that cone-like contraption they used at the end of 'Close Encounters of the Third Kind'. I could imagine an alien spacecraft landing on it at any moment.

My ruminations were interrupted by the entrance of a tall, gliding figure. His entry had been so silent and swift that we were all startled. One bloke was so shocked he nearly punched a hole in his canvas. Apparently this floating apparition was the art historian, who had now stopped and was looking down on us, broodingly, like Caligula. If I said he looked like a Dementor from 'Harry Potter' that would be a bit cruel, but imagine a Dementor that has appeared on 'How to Look Good Naked' and you are getting somewhere close. He had a way of sniffing and putting his nose in the air before he spoke, as if someone had brought in something nasty on the bottom of their shoe.

"Who's first?" he asked, in a voice so refined that it made Brian Sewell sound like Bernard Manning.

Most people tried to hide behind their pictures and the chap who had received such a shock a moment or two before actually got up and bolted out of the room. There was one lady however who bravely stepped forward. The Art-Man put on spectacles and, with a downturn of his mouth, he began to examine her work. We all held our breath and waited for annihilation to come but, after a few moments, Caesar began to make purring noises and his body language visibly thawed. It seemed that he liked what he saw! He began to speak unintelligibly about this woman's painting. Occasionally a word I could understand popped up, like 'medieval' and 'important'.

It turned out that this was a rare and valuable work and after about five minutes the owner went on her way, very pleased.

Eventually, it was my turn. With trembling fingers I held up my tacky effort. The art historian took one look at it and recoiled, like Voldemort about to cast a withering spell.

"Well," he managed finally, "You're obviously happy with it on your wall," (this spoken like I was a carrier of leprosy) "It is clearly the work of an amateur, done at the weekend." He finished with a sniff so loud and prolonged that I thought he might implode. I have never been very confident with art ever since.

Nevertheless, it was to the Lowry Gallery, Theatre and Centre for the Arts, in Salford, that Brian and I were heading - by tram. Historically, Salford has played second fiddle to Manchester and parts of it remain in need of redevelopment. It comes under the umbrella of Greater Manchester although it has its own university and cathedral and now, of course, the notable Salford Quays. This development came about in the 1980s, when the visionaries (and I mean that sincerely) of Manchester and Salford councils set about to rescue the derelict waterfronts of the River Irwell and the Manchester Ship Canal.

The regeneration still continues over twenty years later, but there have been some spectacular advances. There are many buildings of architectural merit springing up. In the 1960s the concrete tower-blocks seemed to me to be plain and ugly but nowadays they can use concrete in all sorts of imaginative ways, resulting in some stunning design. Salford has many fine, new buildings and it is an exciting journey to the Lowry along the quays.

The Lowry was opened in the year 2000. It was designed by Michael Wilford and contains theatres, galleries and restaurants and it is one of the most prestigious venues in the area. If you look carefully at the exterior you can see how the architect has included some of the stereotypical Manchester skyline. There is a gasometer and other large, metallic geometric shapes, which reflect the cranes, the storage tanks and the cooling towers of the industrial era. I suppose that these things were the stuff of Lowry's paintings. The outside of the building has a silver sheen, which attracts reflections and refractions off the water. The whole thing might sound like a bit of a hotchpotch but it works.

If you look across the water southwards from The Lowry you can see Old Trafford and if you look north you can see the newly completed (as of 2011) Media City. It is home to several departments of the BBC and also ITV and, I am sure, will prove a major asset to Salford. Perhaps the bravest move by the BBC has been to move its Breakfast Show north. Some presenters have been spotted trailing around North Cheshire's property hot spots. They may be in for a shock if they are after a bargain!

I hope that they will be happy up north. The BBC has been running counselling sessions for its London-based staff on how to prepare for the move. This probably consists of topics like 'The Do's and Don'ts of Black Puddings' or 'How to Train Whippets'. Some staff may decide not to re-locate!

At The Lowry they were showing an exhibition of the work of French Impressionist painter Adolphe Valette. Valette came to Manchester in the early 20th century to work at the Manchester Art School and one of his pupils was L.S. Lowry. He had a great influence on Lowry, bringing with him all the colour, gaiety and excitement of the Parisian Impressionist scene. You can see in Valette's work the forerunners of Lowry's famous 'Matchstick Men'.

I didn't stop long because it was not of much interest to Brian. In retrospect I should have taken him to a sculpture exhibition instead. I joined Brian on the quay for a coffee and I looked down the Manchester Ship Canal towards the Trafford Centre. The sun was setting in that direction, over the Mersey estuary, and I wondered if any Vikings would sail up today. Actually there were a few. About thirty supporters of Widnes Vikings Rugby League Club were sitting on a nearby wall. They must have been in town to watch their team play Salford City Reds. At that moment a little Austin A35 scuttled, beetle-like, down the road, with the name of its driver, 'Bob', printed in large letters on the windscreen. Next to it was the name of his 'significant other', 'Carol'. Bob glanced nervously at the Viking supporters as he passed them and they responded to a man by raising their beer glasses and chorusing, "Alright Bob!" Poor Bob sunk low in his seat, put his foot down and beetled off as fast as his A35 would take him.

I suppose that the original Vikings would find much to marvel at in modern Manchester, such as the music scene and club scene, the gay village and so on. If all that Manchester is lacking is a beach then be reassured, they are probably working on it as I write!

Chapter 14
The Silly Bugger Hills

'The lean and hungry wolf,
With his fangs so sharp and white,
His starveling body pinched,
By the frost of a northern night.
And his pitiless eyes that seare the dark,
With their green and threatening light'
- The Book of Highland Minstrelry, 1846

One member of my family originates from the far north of the Pennines, on the Scottish border, and so she is never happier than when she is running on the hills. Her requirements are simple and her manner unaffected. She will eat anything, likes to go au naturel and is a faithful and affectionate companion. No, I am not talking about a relation of mine, I mean Meg, our sheepdog. Alright, she does have her faults.

When I said she will eat anything then I mean *anything* – the contents of drains, rancid fat, bird food or her own vomit. She is not what you might call a fussy eater.

Meg loves to run in the hills and, in true sheepdog style, she won't keep her eyes off me when she does. She is always awaiting instructions. Should she round up the sheep? Should she fetch that stick? This obsession lets her down occasionally, like the time she fell in a pond. She was springing along as usual, in some heathery moorland landscape, watching me like a hawk, when she suddenly disappeared behind a tuft of bulrushes. She reappeared seconds later soaked through, because she had fallen headlong into a small but deep dew-pond. I didn't know that dogs could look surprised but Meg certainly did at that moment. In some sense you could call her a 'silly bugger'.

I hope you are not offended by the term 'silly bugger'. In the Pennines it is an inoffensive, almost fond term, in the same vein as the Australians' use of the word 'bastard'. My mother always used to call any comedian that she liked a 'silly bugger'; she was affectionate like that. Wherever you are in the world I find it is always best to check with a local before you use any potentially ambiguous words. For example, if you say to an American that you will 'give them a tinkle', I'm afraid it does not mean you are going to phone them, it means something altogether more earthy!

An ex-colleague of mine used to call the Pennines 'The Silly Bugger Hills'. Intrigued by this description I eventually asked him why.

"Because," he replied, "Only silly buggers live up there."

Why so damning, I wondered? Was he thinking of the weather, or the pollution from dark, satanic mills? Perhaps it was the natives. Did he regard Northerners as people who had just crawled out of the primeval soup, wearing a flat cap and a raincoat? Did they keep ferrets down their trousers and use expressions like 'eeh by gum' all the time? Were they all grimy, gritty and grim?

Well, you would be lucky to find a working mill these days, never mind a dark, satanic one, and as for the pollution, it is not half as bad as it used to be. In the 1950s and 60s the River Irwell in Manchester was so full of chemicals from factory outlet-pipes that it was officially classified as a fire hazard! There is a great painting by Manchester artist David Wilde called 'Steam, Speed and Approaching Smog', which depicts the unearthly chemical glow that used to emanate from the water. Nowadays it is practically bursting with wildlife; swans glide gracefully past Salford Quays, and chub, trout and pike are just some of the species of fish there for the catching.

It was time for Jane and me to resume our tour of the Pennines, heading for 'The Silly Bugger Hills'. We went through the same pantomime of packing and loading and falling out. The car was polished, the dog barked and that was it – 'booked it, packed it and forked off'!

Travelling north from Manchester towards Bowland you come first to the Rossendale Valley where you can find the trickily-named town of Ramsbottom, with its steam railway and gem of a Victorian theatre. This part of Lancashire has often been overlooked by the guidebooks but it is a fascinating area. Ramsbottom is becoming quite a fashionable little place but they have not forgotten their roots - they still have a black pudding throwing competition every year!

There are a lot of places round here with the suffix 'bottom'. As well as Ramsbottom there is Whitewellbottom, Broadbottom and (the fantastic) Scoutbottom. Not only do towns and villages have this suffix but people as well. There are Shufflebottoms, Winterbottoms, Longbottoms, and just plain Bottoms. A friend of mine was at one time director of a small company in Rawtenstall, and he happened to have an employee called Colin Bottoms. This wouldn't have been so bad except for the fact that there was also a John Dix on the staff. These estimable chaps were managers in the same office and frequently had phone calls coming through reception for one or the other of them. Occasionally the overworked receptionist would mix up their first names, and so they became Colin Dix and John Bottoms. When my friend pointed out her mistake she was very apologetic.

"Oh," she confessed sadly, "It's true. I do sometimes get my Dix confused with my Bottoms."

Rawtenstall is not only famous for its preponderance of Bottoms. There survives here a Temperance Bar, the only one still in existence. A Temperance Bar is exactly like a pub but without alcohol. This one is called Fitzpatrick's and it is set up exactly like a public house. It has a bar with wonderful hand pumps that deliver cordials on tap, such as 'Sarsaparilla' and 'Dandelion and Burdock' or the rather ghoulish sounding, 'Blood Tonic'. It has that fresh, rather yeasty smell of a health food shop, and the walls are lined with admonitions against the evils of drink. I always like to look in on it when I am in the area, just to see what I am missing.

The bar was opened in 1890 by the Fitzpatrick family, with the worthy aim of preserving the working man from drunkenness and depravity. Malachi Fitzpatrick was the last member of the family to run the bar and he lived till he was ninety - a good advert for the efficacy of his abstemious lifestyle. It was the Temperance Society that was the inspiration behind the bar and it had its origins in Preston in 1832. To begin with it was enough to deny oneself spirits to become a member but soon 'total abstinence' from alcohol was insisted upon and the requirement to 'take the pledge'. It is said that the word tee-total came from a gentleman with a stammer who wanted to take the pledge but who could only manage to say "tee-tee-tee-total abstinence."

I love the accent round this part of Lancashire, with its rich, rolling 'r's (a dodgy phrase I know). The actor Jane Horrocks comes from Rawtenstall so you'll probably know the accent I am talking about. Someone I know from nearby Chorley was once at a bar in London and asked for a cork. Puzzled, the bartender kept asking her to repeat the question. Eventually he gave her a cork from a wine bottle. She walked away embarrassed because what she had wanted was a bottle of that extremely famous cola drink! Those 'rolling 'r's get everywhere.

Rossendale gives way to some pleasant rolling country, with interesting attractions to see. There is Pendle Hill, (of witch-hanging notoriety) and below it little villages like Padiham and Sabden. There is a proper 'pie and peas' cafe here, which I visited once whilst waiting to collect 'Auntie'. She had been to a coachbuilder's to have her front-end restored. (If my Auntie Doreen is reading this then she must reassure herself that I am talking about my car). I mention pie and peas not because it is still a common meal but because, contrariwise, it is so rare. I went into the tiny cafe, where there was just one table, and ordered my pie and peas. There was a simple gingham tablecloth with a little vase of peonies on it. The lady owner was pleasant and talkative and there was an unhurried air about the place. Of course, the pie and peas was magnificent. If this unpretentious establishment had been in Spain or Italy we would be raving about its rustic charms and what not but, because it is in Lancashire, I don't imagine that will happen. You get the same thing with Black Pudding. Restaurant reviewers wax lyrical about the charms of Boudin Noir, which is essentially a blood pudding, but call a thing Black Pudding and people turn up their noses and recoil in horror!

In Clitheroe there is a large and sophisticated wine merchants called 'Byrne's', which has won many an award and featured on TV programmes as august as Jancis Robinson's, but its proprietors still talk with broad Lancashire accents. Your mind does a double-take as you hear them talking learnedly about wine. Surely no-one with such an accent could know things like that…could they?

On the other hand, if you have a public school accent this can cause problems for native speakers. The sister of a friend of ours used to work in a general store in Rawtenstall. One day a lady with a very far-back accent came into the shop and asked for 'Bovril'. Unfortunately, the assistant misunderstood her diction.

"Bog roll?" she replied. "It's over there in the toiletries."

Clitheroe has a castle to look at and, if you visit in August, there is a thriving food fair, where you can sample the produce of the best local chefs. You can get good modern cuisine in the Pennines you know! Quite a large percentage of the populations of Clitheroe and Colne are Catholic and this accounts in part for the presence of the famous public school Stonyhurst College, which is sited between the two towns. Stonyhurst is a Catholic school and moved to these premises in the 18th century from France, via Holland, after religious persecution in those countries forced them out. Thank goodness we have a tradition of tolerance here. The illustrious alumni include the poet Gerard Manley Hopkins, Sir Arthur Conan-Doyle and JRR Tolkien, who was a visiting teacher at the school.

This does give me a very tenuous connection with them all. When I first worked in Sheffield the chap who is now headmaster of Stonyhurst was deputy head at my school. He had interviewed me for my job and one of the questions he asked me was:

"What do you expect from the Independent Sector?"

What I came to expect was the exquisite politeness demonstrated by the pupils, opening doors for you and thanking you for their lesson. But I was less prepared for the often slightly eccentric behaviour they exhibited. Shortly after being appointed I mounted a small dramatic production for the younger boys to be performed for parents at the school's centenary celebrations. It was a modest success and as a 'thank you' to the boys I bought them some sweets to share. Imagine my surprise the next day when I became aware of a 'hem-hemming' noise behind me and turning around found a very small boy about to address me, formally. For the purposes of this story it must be understood that I was wearing a leather jacket. The boy placed the back of one hand to his mouth in the manner of an old-fashioned butler and the other behind his back.

"Excuse me, sir," he began, with all the gravity of Jeeves addressing Bertie Wooster. "I think I speak on behalf of all the boys in wishing to thank you for the bag of toffees which you provided for us. And, by the way sir," he continued confidentially, "I do think you look good in leather."

He turned and strode off, still formally, leaving me open-mouthed and wondering if, after all, single-sex education is for the best.

We 'popped in' to Stonyhurst as it was having an Antiques Fair, and I thought I might bump into the headmaster. The drive is long and very grand, bordered as it is by statuary, and the hall is even grander. On its oak-panelled corridors noticeboards announced competitions for things like 'Rhetoric' and 'Polemics' – this was a heavyweight school. As it happened, the head was nowhere to be found so we continued on our journey.

After you clear the last clinging tentacles of Greater Manchester you come to an area known as the Forest of Bowland and here lies the first clue to solving our mystery about silly buggers. You see, there is no forest there! Above the natural barrier of the River Ribble the Pennines rise steeply again to one of the most remote and bleak areas of England. By no means is it a wasteland - it is actually very beautiful, but there are no forests. There are a lot of bogs, however, and it is unwise to wander off from the beaten track. From time to time people do just that and some of them are never seen again…silly buggers.

Despite its lack of trees the Forest of Bowland seems to retain the title. It is a quiet, you might even say overlooked, area. If it were further north, in the Lake District or the Yorkshire Dales, then people would probably make more of a fuss about Bowland. Perhaps they 'take the huff' when they can't find a forest. Whatever the reason, the region remains fairly isolated.

I suppose the wolves went when the forest went. This was one of the last places in England where wolves were to be found. They died out some time in the mid 15th century, the very last one being killed in the grounds of Wormhill Hall. Before you say 'Ahh' and pull a sad face let me quote a little more of the poem at the beginning of the chapter:

'He climeth the guarding dyke,
He leapeth the hurdle bars,
He steals the sheep from the pen,
And the fish from the boat-house spars,
And he digs the dead from out the sod,
And gnaws them under the stars'

Wolves were a bit of a nuisance weren't they? They were plentiful in the Pennines generally, and in the Forest of Bowland in particular, and proved to be something of a challenge to get rid of before the invention of the gun. Also, they didn't suffer from 'island dwarfism' like many British mammals and as a consequence they were enormous. No doubt they grew fat on all the dead from various battles and from the fact that medieval life tended to be 'nasty, brutish and short'. The wolves must, quite literally, have had 'a field day'.

Many lords had official wolf hunters, and wolf skins were highly prized for their warmth and durability. The infestation of wolves became so intense at times that convicted criminals had their sentences commuted on condition they presented a tribute of so many wolf tongues annually. There is talk of re-introducing wolves to certain areas of Britain. Before they do I hope they reinforce the security around cemeteries!

We had to travel over the Bowland Fells to reach a little village called Dent, where we had booked lodgings. We didn't see any wolves, or forest, but Meg had a good time running around, whenever we stopped for a walk. Dent lies just on the northern edge of Bowland, not far from Kirkby Lonsdale, near the Lake District and the Yorkshire Dales. We passed through Slaidburn, a village so wet that it appeared green with the thick moss that clung to the stone walls and roofs. The pub here is called 'Hark to Bounty', after a comment made by some old squire in the 19th century. He meant that he could hear his dog 'Bounty', barking loudly outside. It was formerly known as 'The Dog Inn'.

Travelling on over the high and deserted fells we eventually reached the north of the region and then started to descend once again into gentler countryside.

We came to the River Lune and the town of Kirkby Lonsdale, which is just in Cumbria. I did get a little shiver down my spine as I arrived because my surname, 'Lancaster', comes from this area. It is a corruption of the word 'Lune-castra', where 'lune' refers to the River Lune and 'castra' the name given by the Romans to a military camp.

"Perhaps my forbears were in the Roman army," I wondered aloud to Jane.

"You certainly have the nose for it," she laughed (for a trifle too long).

Kirby Lonsdale stands on a bluff above the river and right at its heart is St Mary's Church, noted for its fine carved columns. The church was open when we arrived, which is an increasingly rare occurrence, and entering I experienced, as is usual for me in such places, a sense of reverence and peace, mixed with a tinge of regret - I'm not sure why. I reflected on the dozens of generations of people who had worshipped here and invested the place with their hopes and fears. It was quiet and (maybe) watchful, but well worth the visit.

On the edge of the graveyard is the famous 'Ruskin's View', so named after John Ruskin who designated it one of the finest views in England. The aspect is over the River Lune, which snakes languorously across a vivid green floodplain, far below, fringed by comely wooded hillsides. No wonder Turner painted it. I thought that this might be the exact spot where my ancestors hailed from -'the camp overlooking moon-river'.

It was a very sentimental moment but, as a tear formed in my eye, I became aware of Jane tugging excitedly at my sleeve. She confronted me with an unusual request.

"Come over here," she said enthusiastically, pointing in the direction of the cemetery, "there's an oesophagus I want to show you."

My mind jumped at the thought of how they must deal with the newly buried in this town, but then of course I realised that she meant a 'sarcophagus'. I suppose that 'tomb' would be a better word for what she was pointing at but at least it was not the scene of a devilish abomination.

We had a spot of lunch at 'The Orange Tree' and then left for our final destination that day. Travelling north and west we took a minor road to the village of Dent. It meandered beside little woods and rivers, small stone farms and views of distant hills, until Dent could be glimpsed, resting quaintly in a saw tooth-shaped fold of the valley, or a 'dynt' in Old English.

As we drove into Dent it reminded me of a typical French village, unchanged since medieval times. It was not gentrified, sanitised and twee, like so many of our old places, and it was not overrun with cars. The cobbled street and hay barns right in the centre gave it the air of a working village, with a church, two pubs and a shop, all situated snugly along the winding, through road. Holding pride of place amongst the other buildings was a timeless and welcoming hostelry, with a large and elegant pub sign announcing its wares and, as it happened, our destination for that night.

Like the rest of Dent the pub, and indeed its occupants, seemed to be 'ancient of days'. The landlord was sitting by the fire in the bar as we walked in. On seeing us he jumped up immediately and roared, "Yes, sir?" in a way that made it sound like he was going to tear us limb from limb. If his voice was alarming then his appearance did not do anything to allay it. He was small with wiry, white hair that stuck out at angles, and a face that expressed some permanent shock. Many people are put off by this slightly challenging type of approach, but it is really just the Yorkshire way and should be confronted in kind.

"We are staying here for Bed and Breakfast!" I announced, in as confrontational way as I could muster. The landlord looked slightly chagrined and glanced at his watch to see if we were too early (and could therefore be eaten alive!).

"All-reet," he grumbled, "I'll show you to your room."

He led us up some creaking stairs and along a landing before indicating a bedroom.

"Bathroom's down corridor," he yelled, jerking his thumb at a gloomy passageway to the side. "All-reet?"

This seemed to conclude our business and he headed off back to the bar, leaving us to contemplate our fate.

You may remember that after the war about three million tons of a green paint called Eau de Nil was foisted on the nation as army surplus. Every public building from hospitals to libraries seemed to be covered in this sickly coloured substance but I hadn't seen it for many a year. Now, just when the sense of wartime deprivation had left me, here it was in all its glory, covering the walls and ceilings of the bedroom. Not only that but, to complete the theme, it had been painted on top of woodchip! Lying back on the bed I had to close my eyes quickly so as to avoid feeling nauseous from staring at it. But it wasn't the décor or the creaking and sloping floor that was exercising my good wife.

"No en suite!" she remarked, icily. "You knew about that didn't you?"

"Err….."

"But you went ahead and booked it anyway. And why?"

"Well…"

"Because it was cheap, that's why!"

I resisted the temptation to make a joke about the fact that I am from Yorkshire stock and in an attempt to reassure my better half that sharing a bathroom might not be so bad I ushered her onto the landing, to peer in its general direction. As luck would have it, just at that moment a man appeared out of the gloom having just showered, wearing nothing but a small towel. We stared at him as he attempted to cover his embarrassment.

"Afternoon," we chorused cheerfully, feeling rather like voyeurs, but he ignored us and hurriedly shuffled past.

After that we decided that a brisk walk might clear the air and resolved to ask the landlord about routes. He could still be heard in the bar below, bawling at his customers, so we descended the stairs to accost him.

"Landlord, is there a public footpath along the valley?" I enquired (suitably bluntly I thought). He stared at us for a moment as if he was thinking of drawing a knife, and then pointed wildly towards the ceiling.

"You want to walk up to the 'Occupation Road'," he bellowed.

"The Occupation Road...?"

"Yes, you know, the Roman Road - though it's a bit of a haul up there."

Wanting to announce my Yorkshire credentials I piped up,

"Will I still be living when I get to the top?"

A ghost of a smile crossed over his face as he answered, quite quietly for him,

"That depends on your legs!"

The atmosphere thawed and became a little warmer for this banter, and I knew that I had made the correct response!

The path started behind the pub and quickly became a steep track which followed waterfalls past an old lime kiln up to the Roman Road or, as the landlord had called it, the 'Occupation Road'. I reflected on the unchanging mindset of such areas that folklore would still know this two thousand year-old work of the Romans as the 'Occupation Road'. Come to think of it didn't the Roman Ninth Legion go missing somewhere round here?

The path climbed up Flinter Gill and as the trees gave way to moorland we had spectacular views over Dentdale and Deepdale. Near the top is an old stone barn which is the unlikely setting for a museum of agricultural implements, showing the history of how the land has been farmed over the years. Outside is a wooden seat inscribed to the memory of some sadly deceased rambler, placed to take advantage of the stunning scenery. I became quite excited when I discovered what looked like shards of some ancient pottery lying on the ground, thinking that this might be some Roman relic (and we would be rich!). However, closer inspection revealed it to be much more modern and it occurred to me that it might have been an urn containing ashes, which had been scattered round and about. Is it too much to speculate that these were the last remains of the poor chap memorialised on the bench, now present eternally in some sense, in that tranquil and beautiful place?

It was getting towards dusk now and we headed back to the pub, where we spent a very pleasant evening sitting by the fire in the bar, drinking good beer and being entertained by the banter of the landlord and the pub regulars.

Later that night, having retired to bed, I was awakened from a deep sleep by a strange noise. It was quite a loud, gurgling, clanking sound, and in the dark my imagination began to play tricks. Perhaps some time during the long history of this pub there had been troubled souls staying here and black deeds had been performed in the covering darkness. Childhood fears re-emerged and suddenly, wanting the toilet and not daring to tiptoe down the corridor to the bathroom, I panicked and weed in the washbasin. At that moment the clanking, gurgling sound began again and it was coming from the plughole! It dawned on me that it was not some unquiet spirit that was manifesting itself but the pub's antiquated plumbing system. I slunk back to bed hoping that no one would guess my guilty secret and was reassured by similar gurgling coming through the pipes from other rooms.

The rest of the night didn't go to plan either. Apart from wanting value for money, another good reason for choosing this place was that it allowed dogs in the bedrooms. I should have learned, after the events in Huddersfield and from other previous experience. Some years ago we had taken a young sheepdog, called

Ben, to a hotel in the Lake District. He was still an adolescent, quite nervy, and only part trained. Every little noise from outside the room made him growl or bark. But, he was very quick to learn and so when he saw me using the en suite bathroom he thought that this must be for him too and promptly cocked his leg on the toilet bowl.

I think I mentioned earlier that Jane has been known to sleep walk. These events don't happen often and don't last long but at the time they can be quite alarming. I was just drifting off again after the disturbing toilet incident when Jane suddenly leapt in the air like a mad-woman, shouting indecipherably. She marched around the bedroom, like Lady Macbeth confessing to the murder of Duncan, and then, just as suddenly, collapsed on the bed and carried on sleeping. My eyes flicked open wide and my brain tried to unscramble what was happening. This was not unusual I said to myself, I could cope.

What I had not foreseen was the effect of the night-light and of the dog. We often take one of those plug-in night lights with us when we are away and now it was casting its baleful green beams up the wall next to the bed. This too I could cope with. What really spooked me though was the dog. She had woken up with all the noise and now padded quietly between the night light on one side of the room and the space I was staring wearily into. Before my very eyes the green shadow of a large wolf passed silently across the wall. Now it was my turn to leap out of bed.

Eventually I nodded off, but for the rest of the night I dreamed of were-wolves. I suppose that all three of us are most probably silly buggers.

When it was time for breakfast we creaked down said ancient stairs and into a small ante-room off the public bar. Tiny tables had been laid, all in a row, each in front of a long settle. One other couple were eating, rather timidly, as we arrived and I realised that one of them was the bloke we had caught 'in flagrante' on the landing.

"I didn't recognize you with your clothes on," I quipped (rather cleverly I thought) but he just looked down and continued with his breakfast. Having a settle meant that we had to sit next to one another and the tables were so small that any sudden movement with a knife and fork meant that you were in permanent danger of impaling your dining companions.

After a few moments a shuffling noise was heard and a stooping figure clutching a notepad and pen entered. This proved to be the landlady, who was unusual in that she walked at an angle, as if into a force eight gale, with an expression preoccupied yet distant. She fixed the other guests with eyes that seemed larger than life, thanks to huge and very thick glasses.

"Have you emptied?" she queried obscurely.

The other two froze like rabbits in a headlight, toast poised halfway to mouth. The various possible meanings of this question worked silently around their faces until further illumination came.

"Your rooms …have you emptied your rooms yet? Oh, never mind."

She disappeared, muttering, in the direction of the bar, at a forty-five degree angle. A little later, as we tucked into our (very good) Full English, I asked politely if there might be the possibility of some toast. The landlady stopped in her tracks and her distant look became pained.

"I forgot it," she confessed, and then continued in an accusatory way,

"It's probably burning now!"

Turning on her heels she sloped off, presumably to rescue the wretched toast.

Later, as I was paying our bill on the landing (strangely, the place they kept the credit card machine), I managed to snatch a few final words with the landlord.

"I notice," I began, "that the postcode here is for Cumbria, and yet the local signs say Yorkshire Dales. Which county are we actually in?"

I might as well have put an electric charge through him or put dynamite under his feet. He pulled himself up to his full five feet six inches, hair on end as though clutching a Van De Graaff generator, and an expression which suggested that he might easily have disposed of the Ninth Legion single-handed.

"This is Yorkshire!" he hissed, through clenched teeth. "Damn Ted Heath and the boundary reforms of the 1970s!"

I took my credit card receipt nervously and tried to make light of the situation.

"Well," I managed, "we're off to Haworth this morning," and then I backed quickly down the stairs and fled, pausing only long enough to mutter over my shoulder,

"Silly bugger!"

Chapter 15
One of our Brontës is Missing

*'Haworth expresses the Brontës; the Brontës express
Haworth; they fit like a snail to its shell'
- Virginia Woolf.*

There are a lot of snails in Yorkshire. It's the damp
they like. There's the Dun Snail, and the Mouse
Ear Snail – they are both Salt-Marsh Snails and can be
found over on the Humber Estuary. Then there's the
Mountain Whorl Snail and (my favourite) the Whorl
Wall Snail. Altogether there are more than thirty
species and approaching 45,000 snail sites on record -
according to the Yorkshire Conchological Society. But
why did Virginia Woolf compare the Brontës and
Haworth to the symbiotic relationship between a snail
and its shell?

We were not actually staying in Haworth but in Skipton. The idea was to catch the usual train from Skipton to Keighley and then take the steam train to Haworth. We had travelled down from Dent, passing under the arches of one of the magnificent viaducts on the Settle-Carlisle Railway, and drove into Skipton to look for our hotel.

During the credit crunch of 2009 the BBC dispatched a reporter to Skipton, to see how the provinces were coping. Those who have been to Skipton will know it to be a prosperous market town, founded largely on agriculture. I once observed an old farmer in a pub here ordering a plate of liver and onions. He was wearing a trilby hat and a battered tweed jacket. After he had pulled a face at the price he pulled a fat roll of fivers out his pocket to pay. They were contained by a straining elastic band and the farmer licked his fingers before peeling a couple off. Folk do alright in Skipton!

The reporter accosted a lady in the town square and asked her, rather pityingly, how Skipton was managing the financial crisis. Retaining perfect composure, she replied, in an understated way,

"Oh, fine thank you very much….I understand that you are having a little difficulty in London."

Skipton has a large market square overlooked at one end by a medieval castle, which is still privately owned. It has some excellent food shops and some excellent pubs, my favourite being 'The Woolly Sheep'- because it serves the full range of 'Timothy

Taylor's' beers. The castle is owned by Lord Clifford and it has been in his family since it was constructed, in 1310. One of the highlights in its illustrious history is the fact that the Cliffords and their men held out against Cromwell's troops for three years during the English Civil War. The walls of the castle are six feet thick and they are intersected by six enormous turrets. The whole place was too strong to defeat. When the civil war was over Cromwell was so annoyed with the indomitable fortress that he ordered it to be 'sleighted' or, in other words, rendered indefensible. They are tenacious in Yorkshire.

I always enjoy visiting Skipton. People chat in the town square; the market traders sit and watch the world go by, and colourful narrow boats chug along the canal; it is a happy place. There is a sweet little train station with a similar air of contentment about it; it was the perfect place to start a journey to Haworth.

I was very excited about the prospect of a journey by steam train. Has there ever been a more glorious British invention than the steam locomotive? I would like to claim that it was invented entirely in the North but that would be a step too far. Certainly it was developed largely in the North, by George Stephenson and his ilk, but it is Cornishman, Richard Trevithick, who can lay first claim to its invention. He travelled to Newcastle to work with mine engineer George Stephenson, and it was Stephenson with his son Robert who founded the world's first locomotive-building company in 1825. Railways really took off (not literally) in 1829, with the famous Rainhill time trial at the opening of the Liverpool to Manchester Railway. The owners of the line had been wondering whether to have a standing steam engine that pulled wagons using cables, or whether to have a steam locomotive. A competition was duly arranged and several locomotives took part, including Stephenson's 'Rocket'.

The time trials were a major event of national interest, watched by large crowds, including many business people and politicians. In fact, the Prime Minister himself, the Duke of Wellington, headed up the celebrities. Betting books were opened and on the day the majority of gamblers placed their money on the locomotive 'Novelty', which had become the favourite.

When you read accounts of the race it sounds like a scene from that wacky film of the 1960s, 'Those Magnificent Men in Their Flying Machines'. You can imagine the splendid Regency gentlemen standing around taking a punt on the outcome. Perhaps the Duke of Wellington had his telescope out and was making comments like,

"Dammit sir, you've lost your leg."

There were five engines altogether competing for the £500 prize and the contract to supply locomotives to the Liverpool and Manchester Railway Company - and they were an extraordinary bunch. There was 'Perseverance', which looked like a giant milk bottle on wheels; 'Novelty', which resembled a mobile brewery;

'Sans Pareil', the very epitome of a modern car exhaust system; 'Rocket', which at least looked something like a prototype of a modern steam locomotive and (the most exotic) 'Cycloped', which was powered not by steam but by a horse running on a conveyor belt attached to a wagon.

The whole lot looked like they had been designed on the back of a fag packet by the people on those mad TV adverts for Guinness. All had to be fed with copious amounts of coal, except for 'Cycloped', which had to have access to a regular supply of hay.

It was 'Cycloped' that failed first. The horse bravely tried to move the contraption it was strapped onto but it panicked and, breaking into an unexpected gallop, smashed through the floor of the wagon, ending up with its feet on the railway track. Next to go was 'Perseverance', which had been damaged in transit and never lived up to its full potential; it received a £25 consolation prize. Another two of the engines more or less blew up, having cracked cylinders and burst pipes. This left only 'Rocket', which performed reliably over several trials, reaching a top speed of thirty miles per hour. It must have been a fine sight, powering down the line and showering the crowd with flaming cinders, due to a faulty smoke box. The Stephensons were awarded the £500 prize and the contract to run the service, despite the fact that their locomotive ran over and killed Liverpool MP William Huskisson at the official opening of the line several months later.

The original 'Rocket' now stands in the Science Museum in London (where else) but you can see a replica at the National Railway Museum in York. Better still you can take a ride on a replica of 'Planet', 'Rocket's' sister, at Manchester Museum of Science and Industry. The trip uses a section of the railway line where the 1829 trials took place and also goes right over the set of Coronation Street! Incidentally, there is another interesting steam train in the York museum, namely 'The Hogwarts Express', from the Harry Potter films. The steam railway at nearby Goathland on the North York Moors was used for one of their locations.

Today we were going on the Keighley to Worth Railway, which stops at Haworth. Keighley station is a hybrid, where the national rail network meets a private steam railway. It took me right back to my childhood because it resembled the model railway I used to have as a boy. The bridges over the track were the same and the design of the canopy over the platform was the same. Even the fencing was a scaled-up version of the picket fence I used to attach to the side of the track.

Keighley and Oakworth stations were used as a location for the film 'The Railway Children', and so was the line to Haworth. In 1970, when the film was made, this was the only private steam railway in the country that possessed a tunnel of sufficient length for the purposes of the story. In addition, the line passes through some lovely countryside, which is probably best viewed on film and not with your head sticking out of a train window. This is partly because of the risk of losing your head as the train plunges into a tunnel, but also because if you are down wind of a steam engine then you tend to get grit in your eye and soot all over your face.

I was already starting to look like a windswept version of Dick Van Dyke in Mary Poppins but what kept me going was the fact that, as far as I know, this train is the only one ever to have achieved an entry in 'The Good Beer Guide'. It has an amazing buffet carriage, complete with a bar and draught beer. Various drinkers were installed on bar stools and we soon had a good conversation going between us. The only downside was that when the train went over points or tilted going round a bend the beer tended to travel in vertical or horizontal directions of its own choosing, not necessarily into one's mouth.

It is a long haul from Haworth station up to the former Parsonage where the Reverend Patrick Brontë lived, with his children Charlotte, Emily and Anne, in the 19th century. His title was 'Perpetual Curate', a position he kept for over fifty years, until his death at the age of eighty-four. I suppose we were travelling in the footsteps of tens or hundreds of thousands of others who have made this pilgrimage. One of the most notable has to be Virginia Woolf, who travelled here from London in 1904, to do articles for the Manchester Guardian and the Times Literary Supplement. It is an interesting account to read from a perspective of more than one hundred years distance and it included the quote at the beginning of the chapter about the Brontës and snails.

It is not only living snails that Yorkshire can boast in plentitude but fossils of snails, and of many other pre-historic creatures. The coast from Staithes to Flamborough contains stone ferns, flowers, lizards, crocodiles and even stone dinosaur footprints. Only one dinosaur skeleton has been found in Yorkshire. It is of the hadrosaur subspecies, the ones that might just possibly have been dragons!

However, there is one missing dinosaur that used to feature significantly in my childhood. This is because it now no longer exists by the same name. Do you remember those enormous vegetarian dinosaurs with long necks and tails, but with a relatively tiny head? They were called Brontosaurus weren't they? Not anymore apparently. They are now called Apatosaurus for reasons that escape me. Brontosaurus is 'scientifically redundant'. Could this be our missing Brontë?

I have to say that Virginia Woolf, great writer though she is, does come across as a tad supercilious about Yorkshire in general and Haworth in particular – in a way that (hopefully) you wouldn't find these days. She describes it as 'dingy and commonplace', with buildings of 'ugly, yellow-brown stone'. The words 'blot' and 'landscape' are also used in proximity to each other.

On the contrary, we found Haworth to be charming. It has attractive cobbled streets, with houses and shops of a warm, weather-worn texture that spill onto the cobbles in a cosy, intimate jumble. Halfway up the hill from the station the road forks around a lovely wedge-shaped terrace of houses, and where it forks it makes a small impromptu town square. On your left is the old 'Black Bull' which was a pub in the Brontës era. Sadly, they would probably only recognise it from the exterior these days, as inside it has been ripped apart by the 'progressive' pub company that owns it.

Next to the pub is St Michael's Church. The only part of *this* that the Brontës would have recognised is the 17th century tower. All the rest was demolished and rebuilt in 1879 by Patrick Brontë's successor as vicar. Unlike the pub chain next door he may have had good reason. In 1850, the same year in which Charlotte Brontë was writing an introduction to a new edition of 'Wuthering Heights', by her recently deceased sister Emily, an official from the 'General Board of Health' was undertaking a study of the sanitary conditions prevailing in Haworth at that time. He discovered that the town had only sixty-nine privies, or one for every four houses. In addition there was no proper drainage system, which meant that the drinking water supply was being contaminated with effluence. What is worse, he discovered that the modest graveyard contained the remains of over 40,000 people, stretching back over two hundred years. The graveyard was sited at the top of the town and this resulted in putrefying remains seeping downhill into the town wells. No wonder the average life expectancy was only twenty-four years, and that more than forty per cent of children died before the age of six. The Brontës were dying young, but they were living the normal life span for Haworth.

A somewhat gross addition to this story is the fact that the 1850 study found that rotting substances were actually being absorbed by the walls of the church, as some kind of ghoulish damp problem. The smell must have been appalling, and the actions of the new vicar not only understandable but long overdue.

Just behind the churchyard stands the Parsonage, now the Brontë Museum. It was to this place that Rev Patrick Brontë brought his wife, Maria, and young family in 1820. Patrick had the unenviable lot of bucking the trend and outliving his wife and his six children, as well as his sister-in-law. They all died of tuberculosis apart from Maria, who probably had stomach cancer. One can only speculate what this must have meant to him to watch his vivacious and gifted family leave him one by one. Perhaps Virginia Woolf spoke with intended irony when she remarked rather sniffily of the Yorkshire weather,

"I understand that the sun seldom shone on the Brontë family."

I am sure that most readers of this book will have read some of the Brontës works. If not, then most likely you will have seen film adaptations of 'Wuthering Heights' or 'Jane Eyre'. If you have failed to do even that then you might have come across them in the music of Kate Bush. Actually, there have been many classical compositions, including a cantata and an opera based on their work, as well as several film scores.

Wuthering Heights and Jane Eyre have attracted the majority of the adaptations. In the 1939 Hollywood version of Wuthering Heights a handsome Lawrence Olivier as Heathcliff, woos Merle Oberon's Cathy (using beautifully-clipped vowel sounds). David Niven, who played a rival suitor, recalls the director asking him to act more emotionally as he knelt over Cathy in her deathbed scene. He tried really hard to make himself cry but only succeeded in making snot come down his nose, all over the 'patient', at which point the barely breathing Cathy screamed, leapt out of bed and ran out of the room.

Virginia Woolf was not overly impressed with the Parsonage Museum either, calling its contents 'pallid and inanimate', although she did find pathos in the meagre personal possessions of Charlotte, such as her 'thin muslin dress'. The things here that made the most impression on me were the tiny bound notebooks that the sisters wrote in, only two and a half inches by one and a half! Their handwriting was minuscule and requires a magnifying glass to decipher.

Paper must have been precious to them, as were all their few possessions probably. There was no 'conspicuous consumption' for them. They suffered privations and deprivation, but they remained strong. Maybe they did inhabit a narrow world geographically, but they also inhabited a world of love and affection – a creative world, driven by intelligence, mutual support and artistic ambition. Certainly, their written legacy has enriched our language and literature but their lives also speak to us. Charlotte's tribute to her two sisters, Emily and Anne, contains the following affecting passage:

'In Emily's nature the extremes of vigour and simplicity seemed to meet. Under an unsophisticated culture, inartificial tastes, and an unpretending outside, lay a secret power and fire that might have informed the brain and kindled the veins of a hero. Anne was long-suffering, self-denying, reflective and intelligent. Neither was learned; they had no thought of filling their pitchers at the well-spring of other minds; they always wrote from the impulse of nature, the dictates of intuition, and from such stores of observation as their limited experience had enabled them to amass. For strangers they were nothing, for superficial observers less than nothing, but for those who had known them all their lives in the intimacy of close relationship, they were genuinely good and truly great'.

I think that this passage makes me realise why I am uneasy with Virginia Woolf's Haworth/Brontë snail analogy. The intelligence and greatness that Charlotte attributes to her sisters is also clearly present in her voice. To me snails conjure up sloth, slowness, and a limited outlook on life, which are not words and phrases that sit comfortably with the Brontës.

I wondered if I was looking through 'rose-tinted spectacles' at Haworth compared to Woolf, who came across as so condescending about the North, if not about the Brontës. I decided to do a bit of research to see if I could find some views on the town from recent visitors. As far as I could tell they all loved it. Everything that Virginia found ugly or commonplace the 21st century tourist seems to like. They use adjectives like 'beautiful', 'peaceful' and 'gorgeous', to describe the town. It doesn't sound like the same place at all.

I wouldn't want to suggest that Virginia Woolf was a dinosaur but she does evoke the echo of certain attitudes - ones that carry a faint roaring sound from the Jurassic period! Sadly, I witnessed the same antediluvian tone from the great Brian Sewell in a recent televised discussion about the painter LS Lowry. He was debating Lowry's relative merits and de-merits with the Manchester novelist Howard Jacobson. Sewell maintained that Lowry's earlier work was much superior to his later work because Lowry, being an unsophisticated Northerner, got big-headed about his success and started to show off in his painting. He accused David Hockney of the same fault. I may be wrong but I think this was the gist of his argument.

Sewell pronounced the word 'Manchester' as if he were spitting something unpleasant out of his mouth, which provoked one member of the audience, our fine actor of the soul, Ian Mackellen, to declare his northern credentials. He went on to make some salient points about the greatness of Lowry's later work. To his credit Brian Sewell did back down somewhat at this, and promised to go and look again at the later works, to see if he had missed something.

I suppose you are wondering if the redundant Brontosaurus is our only missing Brontë. Unhappily, there is a more serious one. It is poor Branwell, the only male sibling. He died at the age of thirty from the combined effects of tuberculosis, alcohol, and opium (and probably a broken heart). He died in the attitude of simply leaning against the fireplace! One could speculate how long it took for the others to realise that he was 'no more', because of his lately settled disposition, but that would be an unkind train of thought.

Branwell painted and wrote poetry, but the problem was he was not really as talented as his illustrious sisters, and perhaps that was a frustration for him. When Anne Brontë was tutoring at Thorpe Hall, near York, she invited her brother Branwell to visit. He promptly fell madly in love with the married lady of the house and they started an affair, which lasted for over two years until discovered. Branwell was then banned from the house and area and slipped into a decline from that point on.

It is not known how his father and sisters took the news of this turn of events. Branwell returned to Haworth and remained there. There is no suggestion that he became unloved by his family but there is a clue as to how he felt about himself. He had once painted a portrait of himself standing with his three sisters round a table. The work was serviceable but not really remarkable. It survives to this day and the sad thing is that, at some stage, Branwell painted himself out of the picture. You only see him now as a ghostly outline behind the others. Redundant can be a terrible word.

Chapter 16
Up a Hill Backwards

'The thredend day sal dede mens bones
Be sett to-gyther and rise al attanes' [1]
- The Pricke of Conscience (circa 1400)

I f the Pennines form the backbone of England then the M62 motorway forms the spinal cord. It tracks through the vertebrae of the hills like the image on an MRI scanner; its smooth straight progress belying the appallingly difficult terrain it negotiates.

We were driving south from Skipton to the land of my fathers – Brighouse. We had passed Halifax and had to take in a short stretch of the M62 to reach our destination. The M62 is Britain's highest motorway, at over 1,000 feet, and forms part of a grand

---

[1] On the thirteenth day all the dead shall rise.

intercontinental route that starts at Holyhead on Anglesey, and travels all the way to Ishin in Uzbekistan - not that I have noticed many Uzbeks on this section of the route. You tend to get Rugby League teams and their supporters using it a lot though, travelling east and west to knock seven bells out of each other. The motorway crosses the Pennines, from Manchester in the southwest to Leeds in the northeast but, although it was mooted as long ago as 1945, it did not officially open until 1976, such were the difficulties of funding, planning and building it.

Prior to this the only way over the precipitous moors was on twisting, narrow lanes. I well remember them from my childhood, journeying home past midnight in the fog, after visiting relatives in Brighouse.

We were soon passing Stott Hall Farm, which is a curious anomaly on the M62. At one of the highest points on the motorway the east and west carriageways diverge to accommodate a farm in between the two. This is Stott Hall Farm, which once must have occupied a prime location atop the moors, but which now has its peace shattered by the thousands of vehicles that pass every day. The lorries and cars whiz by, not fifty feet from the front door and, naturally, everybody has a good nosey as they do. It is still a working farm and has special underpasses to take livestock back and forth to pasture. It must be a nightmare living there because the traffic never stops. You wonder why on earth the owners didn't take compensation and find a new, quieter area in which to farm. Being Yorkshire you can probably guess the farmer's reaction when approached by the motorway builders.

"I am not moving from this spot! This farm has been in my family for five-hundred years and it will still be here when the motorway has gone to perdition!"

I suppose the conversation might have gone something like that and finished up with the farmer brandishing his shotgun and chasing the planners away.

In fact, the reason the farm remained and the motorway went around it is because of the awful peaty and boggy land on which it stands. Despite the engineers best efforts to put down a firm foundation the land just kept swallowing up concrete pile after concrete pile, until they had to admit defeat and make a detour. The family continue to live and work at Stott Hall Farm and are now quite famous, having been the subject of several newspaper articles and TV programmes.

Driving along a motorway gives 'Auntie' a chance to prove that she is a modern car. With overdrive in place she can bowl along the road at great speed. Her acceleration is not spectacular but 'keep your foot down' and after about twenty miles you will practically be breaking the sound barrier. 'Auntie' was built in an age when the derestricted road sign meant just that, and she cruises along beautifully at high velocity. Not that I would dream of going too fast in the old girl, as she does suffer from mild arthritis. To be honest there have been three 'Aunties' over the last thirty-odd years. The first one I crashed!

I don't blame 'Auntie', because it was my own fault. I was taking the dog to the vets which, like all dogs, she hated. Dogs seem to know when it is to the vets you are heading, and not for a nice walk. I met a farmer in the pub recently who told me that he has to hitch a trailer full of sheep to the back of his car when he takes his sheepdog to the vets; otherwise the dog guesses where he is being taken and won't get in.

For reasons such as this my dog was jumping around in 'Auntie', in a way that was positively dangerous. Any moment she was going to land on my lap as I was driving. This would have been *very* dangerous so, like a fool, I did something even more dangerous instead. I turned around to the back seat and attempted to secure the dog to a door handle. Of course, this meant that I was no longer looking at the road. When I looked up 'Auntie' had drifted into the opposite carriageway, into the path of an oncoming coach. As his vehicle bore down on me I vividly recall the coach driver's face recording shock and horror at the imminent crash.

The Rover P4 is a car of legendary strength. It is built like the Forth Road Bridge, more on the philosophy of the 'turret top' than the 'crumple zone'. Still, to do battle with a charabanc was a 'big ask'. I yanked the steering wheel to one side and awaited the worst.

Do you believe in angels? I think I saw one at the moment of impact. It was standing between me and the coach, complete with wings and long white robes, holding a flaming sword. Before you put me down as bonkers I hasten to add that I have never seen anything like that before or since. It is easy to explain away psychologically, as the manifestation of an over-heated brain or even as the result of the physical jolt that I experienced, but I like to think that it was because my 'number' was not yet 'up' and that I was meant to live to fight another day.

Whatever the reason, I survived, despite the fact that the car was knocked several feet backwards, up a hill! In fact, the dog and I got away scot-free as did the coach driver, thankfully. The only damage 'Auntie' received was to her front wing, the one that I had been painstakingly restoring, but because of the incident I lost heart with her, and when the opportunity came to swap her for a more pristine 'Auntie' I did so.

It was this 'Auntie' that we were travelling in from Skipton to Brighouse. Not far from Stott Hall Farm the car engine started to miss. Unluckily, I was in the outside lane because I was overtaking a group of vehicles. Somehow I managed to steer across to the hard shoulder where we rolled to a halt, and were left staring at each other whilst the motorway traffic flew past.

"Not again," said Jane. "We are going to have to get a newer car" (plus a few unrepeatable remarks).

I pretended not to hear these comments. I had a contact at a garage in Brighouse so I rang the guy, who turned up fairly quickly with his tow truck. For some reason he was only able to attach a rope to 'Auntie' and so we had to limp into town ignominiously attached to a tow rope. I am sure it is illegal to tow a broken-down car miles along a motorway but we managed it without attracting untoward attention.

The only problem came at a road junction soon after we had left the M62. Some nice driver signalled to let the tow truck out but just at that point a pedestrian tried to cross the road between our two cars. She mustn't have noticed the rope and tripped headlong over it in pantomime style. When she had recovered she became angry and attempted to find pen and paper to take down my details. Meanwhile the mechanic in the truck put his foot on the accelerator to move off, waving and smiling at the kindly motorist who had stopped to let him out. I, on the other hand, was preoccupied with the irate lady who had taken such a Charlie Chaplin-like fall, and kept my foot firmly on the brake. It was the only time I have ever seen sparks fly from the tyres of a vehicle as the tow truck tried to pull a two-ton Rover with the brakes on.

Arriving at the garage in Brighouse the mechanic peered under the bonnet.

"Your plugs are oiled up," he declared. "I'll clean them up for you."

This gave Jane and me just enough time to wander round some old haunts, before collecting the car and heading for Huddersfield, where friends had kindly offered to put us up for the night (and also to take us to see the Huddersfield Choral Society in concert).

I thought of my childhood visits to Brighouse to visit the extended family and reflected that there were hardly any of them here now. They have all moved on, one way or the other. I barely recognised Brighouse as we dawdled through the centre. The factories have mostly gone, like Firth's Carpets or Sugden's Flour Mill, having either been flattened or converted into apartments. The place has become a dormitory town for people who work in Leeds, and posh bars and gastro pubs have sprung up on the high street. There still remain plenty traditional pubs, I am pleased to say, like 'The Yorkshire Bridge' which, commendably, holds a pork-pie competition every month!

Being here again made me feel like Mole in 'Wind in the Willows', in the chapter where he suddenly catches a scent of his old home:

'Home! That was what they meant, those caressing appeals, those soft touches wafted through the air, those invisible little hands pulling and tugging, all one way.'

I thought about the happy family gatherings on Boxing Day with Uncle Reggie taking the role of card-sharp as we played 'Chase the Ace' for pennies. He would deal the cards swiftly and accurately, and

'Auntie'. We found our mechanic trying to turn over the engine with the starting handle.

"Your battery's flat," he grumbled, looking decidedly red in the face.

That generation of motors carried a starting handle for just such emergencies. You have to place this dangerous piece of iron into a trickily small hole in the radiator grille and then yank it as hard as you are able, in a clockwise direction, until the engine fires. It sounds simple enough but it is an operation fraught with peril. For one thing you have to keep your thumb out of the way; otherwise, if the engine kicked back you would be liable to break it. Also, the engine generally needs such a lot of 'turns' before it fires that you are likely to suffer a heart attack or a slipped disc attempting it. I moved in to help the mechanic and the pair of us risked injury or death trying to turn over the engine. The air was blue! We both collapsed in a lather of sweat. Suddenly Jane piped up,

"Did you turn off the fuel supply switch when mending the plugs?"

It was a moment both as embarrassing as it was illuminating. Of course, the Rover had a switch to isolate the fuel supply to facilitate safe repairs on the engine. It was illuminating because the mechanic had forgotten about this and run down the battery trying to start the car. It was embarrassing because it was Jane who had solved the problem. If the mechanic's face hadn't already been bright red from exertion it would have turned red from shame!

Halifax lies to the north of Brighouse and Huddersfield lies to the south. If you ask people one fact they know about Huddersfield they usually mention the Choral Society. This world famous choir, which has had works specially composed for it by the likes of William Walton and Ralph Vaughan Williams, was founded in 1836, and is essentially amateur in its tradition, like many of the choirs and brass bands in the North of England.

It is a marvel how such organisations as the Huddersfield Choral Society or Brighouse and Rastrick Brass Band managed to become singers and musicians of professional standing on the world stage. In the 19th century the population of The North was busily engaged in things other than music, like manufacturing cotton and weaving textiles. It was not thought, by the owners of the mills and the upper classes, that their factory workers might possess musical talents, still less aspirations to use them. However, after a long day at the mill groups of workers would meet and practise their music for hours on end, until the sheer quality of their work could no longer be ignored, even by the most exclusive conservatoires in London.

'Auntie' managed to make it to Huddersfield without any further bother and Jane and I met our friends outside the magnificent Huddersfield Town Hall. We were eagerly anticipating our cultural evening because, as Jane remarked,

"We rarely experience eyebrow music."

We were entranced by the performance of Zadok the Priest and other pieces, the grandeur of the music being enhanced by the setting of the hall, with its mighty organ that occupies the whole of one wall. Jane's friend engaged us in conversation at the interval and pointed out the double bass player, whom she happened to know.

"Which one do you mean?" asked Jane, peering into the serried ranks of the orchestra. "That one," re-iterated her friend, "the one with the big violin."

Such cheerful banter entertained us as we chatted at our friends' house later that evening, after the concert. We weren't the only guests staying the night, as the occasion was a celebration of a significant birthday for Jane's friend. The night would have passed uneventfully except for the fact that they had installed an extremely sensitive burglar alarm system in their home. When I needed the bathroom in the middle of the night I had to crawl downstairs on my hands and knees to get underneath the level of the photoelectric sensor, which was eagerly waiting to detect the presence of burglars. This in turn excited the dog, who thought that a great game was about to begin and grabbed my foot in her mouth, at which point I yelled, she barked and we both jumped, thereby setting off the alarm.

I managed to make it up the stairs backwards, without attracting attention and nobody realised what had caused the kerfuffle, but in the morning my back was very painful, and it was all I could do to get out of bed. My back does 'go' this way from time to time, probably the result of doing things like pushing 'Auntie' up hills, or having to use the starting handle. I usually visit an osteopath on such occasions but once, a friend of mine from Rawtenstall had recommended a faith healer to me. He told me of some guy he knew who had healed his wife's bad back by putting his hands on the affected part and praying. They had been on the way to see a certain osteopath, famous in the Rossendale Valley for curing people by hitting them with a piece of angle iron. I imagine you would try anything rather than undergo *that* procedure.

In my mind the jury is still out on faith healing. I suppose that if you believe in God then you must believe that such healing is possible but, equally, maybe He has provided us with gifted scientists and medical practitioners to help us. It is difficult to understand why some people are afflicted with ill health of one sort or another, or why bad things happen to good people, but I choose to keep the faith. It gives me more hope than the thought that I am just a heap of chemicals, born out of chaos and doomed to return to nothingness when I die. (Having a bad back makes me think happy thoughts like this!)

It just so happened that the husband of the other couple who were staying was a registered osteopath. Of course he was miles from his treatment rooms but my need was great and he immediately offered to take a look at my back. He felt up and down my spine and announced cheerfully that he could put me straight in five minutes. The only problem was he had nowhere to operate.

Now, in the middle of the garden stood a stone table tennis table; I had never seen an outdoor one before. Perhaps our friends enjoyed tennis but didn't have enough space for a full size court. The osteopath checked it out and declared that it was ideal for our purposes. In due course I hobbled out to the garden, along with everybody else in the house and one or two interested neighbours. I felt a bit like Aslan being led out to be sacrificed in 'The Lion, the Witch and the Wardrobe'.

"Right," said the osteopath, "drop your pants."

Curtains really started to twitch at this point. I have been practised upon by osteopaths many times and so I knew what to expect - all the twisting and turning and jumping up and down; a bit like de-boning a chicken. But our friends hadn't seen anything like it. They watched open-mouthed as the osteopath worked himself up into a sweat hauling me around the table tennis table. It must have looked like we were having a wrestling match, in a very small, impromptu ring.

The lines at the beginning of this chapter are from a medieval Yorkshire poem called 'The Pricke of Conscience', penned by a hand unknown. They appear on one of a series of windows depicting in stained glass the end of the world, based on the Book of Revelation. Roughly translated they mean:

'The thirteenth day shall dead men's bones be knit together and all rise up whole'.

I did get a great deal of relief from the exertions on the table tennis table and was able to carry on with the holiday. I didn't feel a prick of conscience this time but I was reminded of a recent visit to hospital, when I had had to drop my pants for an injection.

"Did you feel a prick?" asked the nurse after it was all over.

"Well," I replied, pulling up my trousers, "I did feel a bit stupid."

Chapter 17
Park Life

'Cracking cheese Gromit'

I learned a great many Pennine sayings from my parents and I feel as though I ought to record them here for posterity, before they disappear from our collective memory. I made some Norfolk friends laugh on one occasion when their little boy stood between me and the television, blocking my view.

"You make a better door than a window," I said, which is quite a common expression in our family. They all fell about.

"You can't get good ones under," my mother used to say - which is an ironic comment on something that is cheap or of poor quality.

Another of hers was,

"You'll catch something you'll never get rid of," which is a warning against having dirty hands.

If you ate something substantial, like a suet pudding, my father would declare,

"It'll stick to your ribs two years after you're dead!" meaning that it would do you good.

Some of the sayings may be a little 'pithy'. If a person is indecisive he may be referred to as being 'like a fart in a colander'. If you want to warn someone against carrying something very heavy you might say to them,

"Be careful, you'll strain your pooping strings," which is a very evocative expression don't you think?

My Grandma probably wouldn't have approved of such sayings, as she had her own, which professed somewhat loftier ideals.

"Man, love thyself," she used to declare to me solemnly, usually when I was least expecting it.

"Do as you would be done unto," she would intone, making me jump.

Once, when I was a little boy, and happily entertaining myself she suddenly loomed over me and warned me sombrely that,

"A bitter old woman is the Devil's crowning glory!"

If these sayings seem rather weak as you read them, try investing them with the voice of Peter Sallis or Bill Owen from 'Last of the Summer Wine' - that is the milieu in which they should swim. Of course, Peter Sallis is famously the voice of Wallace in the 'Wallace and Gromit' cartoons. He has a warm, friendly voice, like a piece of delicious fruitcake. Wallace has his own sayings, such as 'Cracking cheese Gromit!' or 'It's the wrong trousers!' There was an interesting discussion on the radio recently where it was mooted that adverts about financial matters tend to use actors with northern accents. Perhaps it is the perception that there is something honest and reliable in the northern character. You have only to look at Northern Rock!

The day after my stint on the stone table we were heading down the road to Holmfirth, to an art gallery called Northern Light. It is in part run by some friends of ours and they were having an exhibition. This allows me to name drop for a moment. I knew I was going to meet Nick Park at the gallery, the creator of Wallace and Gromit. Nick was a friend of our friends and he was exhibiting some works himself. Our friends had 'tipped us the wink' that he was going to be there and to be prepared. I had rehearsed a little speech because I knew I would get tongue-tied meeting him.

The gallery was located in an old mill south of Holmfirth and, consequently, it was on a large scale as space was not an issue. All the exhibitors had badges with their names on and we were looking at a picture when one exhibitor came up to us and said,

"Hi, I'm Nick."

I glanced at his badge and it said 'Nick Park'. Now, I don't know if it is because I was star-struck, or just an idiot, but I immediately turned to jelly. Here was a multi Oscar winner, shaking my hand and wanting to know who I was. I couldn't remember. Nick smiled at me helpfully and Jane jabbed me in the ribs. My mouth felt dry, my eyebrows shot upwards and I began to burble some strange version of my speech. I wanted to tell the creator of Wallace and Gromit how much I enjoyed and admired his work, but at every compliment I gave him he just glanced to the side and brushed it off. He wanted to know about me! I couldn't think of one interesting thing to say about myself, or about anything I had ever done. Thankfully, after a minute or so the TV people arrived to interview Nick, and as he walked away I could see in his expressions some of the characteristics of his two most famous creations.

Nick Park comes from Preston and in his animations he brings together some northern stereotypes in an entertaining way. Being a Lancashire boy I am sure he is aware of the rivalry between Lancashire and Yorkshire. I particularly like the scene in 'A Matter of Loaf and Death' where the characters approach the county line with Yorkshire, only to be confronted with a high wall topped by barbed-wire and a sign saying 'Yorkshire Border – Keep Out'.

The BBC comedy, 'Last of the Summer Wine', is set in Holmfirth and its main characters are often to be found 'chewing the fat'. They have existential debates over such trivia as Nora Batty's wrinkled stockings or Compo's wellingtons! This popular programme taps into a wisp of smoke from our social history – that of the self-educated working man. As with music a similar scenario was acted out in other artistic and educational fields in 19th century Britain. Many brilliant people from the North were self-educated or attended night classes, often run by sympathetic academics in their spare time. A tradition for philosophical debate grew up amongst the working classes, centred particularly around Manchester, and the faintest echoes of this phenomenon can be found in characters like 'Foggy Dewhurst' from 'Last of the Summer Wine' (which itself echoes Alan Bennett's 1972 TV drama, 'A Day Out').

There is one unpleasant memory about Holmfirth that lingers from my childhood. In the 1950s there were still some institutions around that had once been workhouses. They had become convalescent homes, geriatric hospitals, or mental hospitals, but the older generation were not convinced. They spoke about the workhouse in hushed, fearful tones. It was still in their living memory. Before the advent of the Welfare State the Workhouse was the place you were sent if you were down and out. There you would be separated from your family and made to do manual work or sewing. Once inside the walls, many never left.

There was one such grim establishment not far from my cousin's house. He and I were playing in the local park once when suddenly he tensed and grabbed my arm. I immediately took on his sense of dread and prepared to face whatever disaster awaited us. Coming down the park drive towards us was a lolling figure. It didn't walk but shambled and rambled along in a seemingly random fashion. It was a man, but not a type of man I was used to. His head fell to one side and his arms groped blindly in the air like an unsettled starfish. He was dribbling and making strange noises. In short, he was a little boy's nightmare.

I am sure that this poor chap was perfectly harmless or they wouldn't have let him wander. In days gone by he would have been called a country booby or a drivelling idiot. Lack of social contact and of opportunity, and a lifetime spent in an institution had probably exacerbated his condition, whatever it was. Maybe he was an epileptic or suffering from some form of cerebral palsy. He was obviously suffering mental impairment as well as physical.

He sort of eyed us and headed our way.

"Don't say anything," hissed my cousin. "Just stand still and let me do the talking."

I couldn't have moved if I had wanted to. I felt rooted to the spot. We waited for his approach. When his voice came it was like a mechanical recording of a learned phrase - a stock response.

"How's your father?" he rambled.

"Alright," replied my cousin.

The chap then mumbled and rumbled before repeating the same question.

"How's your father?"

"Alright," said my cousin again.

I don't know how long this stilted conversation went on. Time seemed to freeze. Eventually, whatever mainspring governed his thinking seemed to move and the man shuffled past us and on, who knows where. It was as if I had been released from a spell and although we continued to play I kept a wary eye out for any return of that strange visitor from another place. My conscience pricks me a little bit when I think of my extreme reaction to this person. He probably had a developed emotional sense and could detect our fear. Maybe if we had shown more understanding instead of treating him as though he were some monster then we could have had a more productive time with him. We were only young though.

Chetham's Library in Manchester isn't the only place in the Pennines you can find Chinese tourists, although this other place of pilgrimage draws more from the spiritual rather than the temporal dimension of life. Not far from Holmfirth is Barnsley. Barnsley sometimes gets a bad press from locals in South and West Yorkshire. Indeed, Sheffield people jest that Barnsley folk are so mean that their war cry is "*How much!?*"

Barnsley may seem an unlikely venue for hordes of Chinese but hordes is exactly what it gets. And they all make for the same venue, 'Boots the Chemist'. You see, there is one famous son at least who generously left the town in the 19th century to proselytise the Chinese nation. Hudson Taylor, the son of a pharmacist from Barnsley, took his Methodism to China and subsequently founded the China Inland Mission. This organisation spread far and wide in China and it is estimated that today there are more Christians in that country than there are people in Britain. Taylor is therefore revered as a great man by many Chinese and they make their pilgrimages to Barnsley to see the place he was born. Recently, Barnsley folk were astonished to see a group of Chinese kneel down, outside Boots on the high street, and kiss the ground. This event became so famous in the area that local poet Ian Macmillan was moved to write a verse or two about it.

Close to the Yangtze River in China, in a little museum in a park, there is a grave marker for Hudson Taylor, who died there in 1905. Originally, it had been put up by Chinese Christians in the Protestant Cemetery, but the cemetery was destroyed during the Cultural Revolution of the 1960s. Nevertheless, after the Cultural Revolution was over the Communist authorities restored and replaced the grave marker of this Christian man, and there it remains - in a park in Guangdong.

Chapter 18
Ample Bosom

'All this visible world is but an imperceptible
point in the ample bosom of nature'
- Blaise Pascal (Pensees, 1670)

'I don't know if I'm supporting
them or they're supporting me'
- Dolly Parton (1973)

The Yorkshire Dales represent the widest point, the centre of the crossbeam on the cruciform shape of the Pennines, reaching towards the Lake District in the west and the North York Moors in the east - a distance of almost 150 miles. Our object for that evening was to make it to a self-catering establishment near Thirsk called Valley View Farm. We had booked this place online, but only after a little hesitation. As you look at the beautiful photograph of the wrought-iron sign for the farm it becomes apparent that underneath the words 'Valley View' it distinctly says 'Ample Bosom'. Now, call me an old pervert but if this didn't stimulate my imagination…!

Hesitating to type 'ample bosom' on the internet I searched around the Valley View website and was surprised to find that the farm not only did self-catering but also ran a lingerie company for ladies of a certain size. The intrigue was irresistible!

We retraced our route north from Brighouse past Bradford, Ilkley (bar t'at) and Bolton Abbey, and then turned east to Blubberhouses.

Blubberhouses is one of those strange-sounding names found a lot in this area. Such names may sound amusing, particularly if you live in the South of England, where there are more Norman names. 'Bluber' is Anglo-Saxon, meaning 'spurting waters' and so Blubberhouses simply means 'houses by spurting waters'. Even today we talk about blubbering, in the context of crying profusely.

Another interesting name hereabouts is Crackpot, meaning 'a cave'. The village of Crackpot stands nearby the delightful sounding Crackpot Hall. Perhaps the way we use 'crackpot' nowadays - for a madman or mad idea - comes from the fact that in times past some social misfits left civilisation (or were driven out), to live as hermits in *caves*. In the process they became isolated, muttering eccentrics, i.e. 'crackpots'!

Northern English names come from several different civilisations, each of which swept away the previous one. The Celts were the first people to live here in the historical era, but there are very few examples of Celtic names remaining, as they were often replaced with Viking ones. Most of them refer to hills such as Pen-y-Ghent, 'the head of winds', or Wharfedale, which means 'winding dale'.

The Romans arrived during the 1st century A.D., but they gave us relatively few names. Such places they did name often had defensive, military associations, such as Lancaster, Tadcaster or Chester, all of which refer to camps or forts. Anglo-Saxons followed the Romans and many of their words still exist, particularly in the Northeast. Hexham is an Old English name meaning 'land taken beside a stream by the younger son of the king', which doesn't sound so snappy in modern English.

The next wave of invaders and immigrants was the Vikings. 'Throp' or 'thorpe' is a Viking word meaning 'an outlying farmstead' - hence Milthrop, Gawthrop, Grewelthorpe, and so on. The strange-sounding Fryup gives its name to a dale on the North York Moors but it has nothing to do with a full English breakfast, it is in fact named after the Norse Goddess, Freya.

The Normans were the most recent settlers and their names can be found in abbeys such as Rievaulx, Jervaulx, or Bretton Priory, as well as amongst the landed gentry, like de Burgh, de Neville and de Longvilliers.

Blubberhouses is worth mentioning for another reason besides its strange name; a reason which might have come straight out of a superhero comic or a Bond movie. All around and about it is moorland, featureless for miles, and also elevated and isolated. What better location for some sort of cutting-edge, top-secret scientific research laboratory? And, lo and behold, as you approach the area you see one! A dozen or so of what appear to be giant golf balls rise out of the boggy heather. They must be nearly one hundred feet high - white, round and with dimples. It is as if you have suddenly become one of 'The Borrowers' and any moment a huge Jack Nicklaus is going to tee off.

The first time you see them you want to swerve the car to a screeching halt, so strange and out of place do they appear. I cannot give too many details because of national security you know, but there they are for any traveller to see - a mass of aerials, military equipment and throbbing power! These great balls are probably part of an early warning system against airborne attack, but they definitely look alien in this ancient landscape. It wouldn't surprise me if one day they took off, circled round, dipped in salute and accelerated away into the stratosphere, hopefully not taking too many Yorkshiremen with them for analysis. You can almost hear one alien addressing another,

"This one is saying, 'Eeh, by gum!' What do you think that means?"

But, no more about this - if I am never heard of again you know why.

To the east and north of Blubberhouses the land gradually levels out until you reach the northwest of the Vale of York. This flat stretch between the Pennines and the North York Moors contains some remarkable places such as Fountains Abbey, the biggest abbey ruin in Britain, and one of the biggest in Europe. In its heyday it was a great centre for the wool trade and its satellite churches extended as far as Norway. You can look at the ruin of the abbey and then spend a happy time in Studley Royal, the large park that surrounds it or, if you want some peace and quiet, at nearby Hackfall Woods.

Horse racing and training are popular pursuits on this flat land and there is a big riding industry centred on Middleham. Middleham also boasts a castle, which once belonged to Richard III, who still enjoys some support round here. A Requiem Mass is said in Middleham Church on the anniversary of his death, at The Battle of Bosworth, in 1485.

If you want a more unusual activity then stop off at the village of Scorton, preferably around the middle of

May, when they hold The Silver Arrow competition. This is an archery contest whose origins can be traced as far back as 1673, in order to hone the skills of English archers. Strangely, competitors are allowed to mark their own score card, and to drink beer, but they are fined £1 for swearing. I wouldn't have thought that archery and beer went together particularly well but maybe it was a useful combination when, in 2008, the guest of honour was the politician William Hague.

This is pleasant, leafy, arable country with little streams and woods and chocolate-box villages, not at all the stereotypical picture of the 'gritty' north. Also, it covers a large area - for Britain. Don't forget that North Yorkshire alone is bigger than any other English county, so allow time to get across it.

The capital of the area is Harrogate, which lies in the Nidd Valley. Harrogate is a spa town that developed in the 18th century and, like Buxton, contains many fine stone buildings. They surround a central strip of parkland called the Stray, which extends right into the centre of the town. In spring it is awash with daffodils, and indeed Harrogate has won awards for its floral displays, not only in Britain but throughout Europe. It has become a centre for conferences and conventions and has done so well for itself that it came third in a recent survey to find the best place to live in the UK.

A Viking Hoard was discovered here in 2007, by a father and his son from Leeds, using a metal detector. It included coins from places as diverse as Uzbekistan,

North Africa, Russia and Afghanistan, which just goes to show how we have always had intercourse with peoples far and wide. The total value of the hoard is said to be over £1M and it went on display in York Museum on August 1st 2010 – which is Yorkshire Day!

One of Harrogate's attractions is the Turkish Baths, of which there are only sixteen still in existence in the country. The Baths has a lot of mosaics and Ottoman-style interior design and, crucially, it manages to avoid most of the dubious practices that these places have a reputation for. I always try and pay a visit to steam rooms wherever I am because they are good for bad backs. Steam rooms are slightly less hot than saunas and you can still carry on conversations in them. As you peer through the mist you have a captive audience and I always confidently regale my fellow steamers with stories. I find it great fun talking to strangers. Why is it that they sometimes stare at me and then back slowly out of the room? Incidentally, don't try long term conversations in a sauna because you will eventually dissolve and become a wrinkly puddle on the floor.

When you do emerge, prune-like, from the Turkish Baths then go and re-hydrate in 'Betty's Tea Rooms'. They are sited on a corner overlooking the Stray and demonstrate all the best virtues of the Victorian tea room. You have the waitresses dressed in bombazine black, offset by frilly aprons and caps. There are the tiered cake stands in the windows, displaying layer upon layer of delicious confections, and all arranged prettily on top of paper doilies. There is a range of teas unparalleled in the history of tea shops. You can get Lapsang Souchong, Orange Pekoe, Earl Grey, Oolong, post-fermented Tea, and teas of every colour under the sun, including Black Tea, Green Tea, White Tea and even Yellow Tea.

Generally, I dislike tea rooms. They have improved marginally since smoking was banned but I still feel uncomfortably on display in them, as though someone has stuck me in the front window to drink my cuppa. Smart ladies gossip on adjacent tables and people hover nearby, willing you to vacate your seat so that they can pounce on it. Ugh! Give me a pub any day.

I actually prefer neighbouring Knaresborough to Harrogate. It is less grand but remains a historical and interesting place. It has a castle that once belonged to Sir Hugh de Morville, one of the knights who murdered Thomas Beckett in Canterbury Cathedral, in 1170. Hugh and the other murderers fled to Knaresborough Castle after they had done the dirty deed.

The River Nidd has created an impressive gorge that bisects Knaresborough and in the crag on one side are some fascinating medieval cave dwellings, which include a chapel and the famous 'Mother Shipton's Well'. The well is actually a stone basin which is fed from above by many dripping lines of water. They ooze out of the porous limestone and as they do they create stalactites that fringe the ceiling of the rock face. Over the years people have placed objects under the slow but steady stream and they have become calcified. You can find hats and gloves, pots and pans, and all manner of items both commonplace and rare, including one of Agatha Christie's handbags!

Mother Shipton was a soothsayer and prophetess who lived here as a troglodyte in the late 15th century. She was apparently hideously ugly but made herself popular by making improbable prophecies in bad rhyming couplets. One of her prophecies predicted the Great Fire of London according to Samuel Pepys, who recorded it in his diary. Like all soothsayers Mother Shipton had to pronounce on the future. Consider this prophecy from the perspective of five hundred years on:

'Carriages without horses shall go,
And accidents fill the world with woe.
Around the world thoughts shall fly,
In the twinkling of an eye.
In the air men shall be seen,
Iron in the water shall float,
As easily as a wooden boat'.

Interesting isn't it?

My abiding memory of Mother Shipton's Well however, is not her insightful predictions of the age to come, but of Jane being sick. We had stopped at a farm for a cream tea and got chatting to the farmer's wife. It was a sheep farm and the time of year when sheep are lambing. Unfortunately, many of them had some sort of disease that made them abort or 'cast' their lambs.

The farmer's wife warned us gravely of this problem as we demolished her delicious scones.

"Is it catching?" I joked.

"Well," she replied, in a less than convincing way, "Not very."

'Not very'! What did that mean? Jane took this to heart and was careful not to eat too much cream but she still became ill. The illness took the form of nausea and dizziness and its fruition came with Jane emptying the contents of her stomach over Mother Shipton's precious well. It is probably petrified by now. I worried long and hard about 'casting-lamb disease' but it turned out that a combination of too many cooked breakfasts, cream teas and chocolate eggs were to blame. You see, Jane loves chocolate and it is not unknown for her to secrete it in all sorts of obscure places. Her sickness was a case of her sins finding her out!

It is a leisurely and relaxing drive from Knaresborough to Thirsk, skirting the Howardian Hills. Follow the brown signs for Darrowby and it will bring you straight into Thirsk's market square. Darrowby and Thirsk are one and the same place: Darrowby being the name given to the town by the writer James Herriot. He practised as a vet in Thirsk and the fame of his books brings tourists from all over the world. When you read the books you discover that Herriot was from Glasgow and that he found the Yorkshire people to be intelligent, possessing a keen sense of humour. When the books were televised

Herriot suddenly appears to be from London, and the locals are depicted as being so stupid and uncivilised that they have probably never even sat on chairs. Brown signs point tourists to the 'James Herriot Museum', the re-named 'Darrowby Arms', and for all I know the James Herriot Chemists or Dentists. Despite all this Thirsk remains true to itself as a Yorkshire sheep and cattle town, with a splendid cobbled square surrounded by some ancient and wonderful inns, like 'The Golden Fleece'.

What cafe could provide one with a lovely oak-panelled room, comfortable sofas and a log fire, such as are to be found in 'The Golden Fleece'? What other establishment but a pub would give one a magnificent meal (for me, not Jane) and as much time as one liked to enjoy it? And where would one go to have this lounge to oneself, apart from one other couple; a couple that one strikes up a conversation with and departs from some time later practically related? (I'm all 'one'd-out' now).

We left 'The Golden Fleece' fully refreshed and prepared for what we knew would be a difficult final stage of today's journey. Hereafter the road east takes a seemingly sheer elevation up Sutton Bank onto the North York Moors. This is not the place to give an extensive geological history of Yorkshire but, suffice it to say that over millennia, eras and aeons it has been flooded by vast oceans, pushed up by mighty continental drifts and scoured by enormous ice sheets, leaving plains, dales or moors depending on the hardness of the stone, plus a fondness for fish and chips.

Sutton Bank rises so suddenly from the gentle plains that it is a real shock to the system to find bleak moorland at the top. It boasts a 1:4 climb with a hairpin bend near the top and it is not to be attempted lightly or without due forethought. Caravans are banned! To attempt Sutton Bank in a 1963 Rover is a triumph of hope over experience and, having been reduced to first gear very quickly, it was only by much lamentation and beseeching of the heavens that 'Auntie' attained the top. At one point I considered getting rid of any excess ballast, such as the dog, or Jane but, being small, she would probably not have made much difference. The views over the dales, the Hambleton Hills and the Howardian Hills are magnificent. You can see Castle Howard (of Brideshead fame) and the Kilburn Horse, a gigantic chalk hill figure.

The hairpin bend near the top adds to the excitement. I heard from a local barmaid that recently a butcher's lorry had deposited its entire load of fresh meat all over the road there. The back doors had not been closed properly and then, sadly, gravity did the rest. The poor driver just sat down and wept as the police began to clear up the now useless sides of beef, strings of sausages and so on.

Finally we made the summit and shortly after were following signs for Cold Kirby, Old Byland and Ample Bosom Farm (I mean Valley View Farm). Old Byland is a small, pretty village near to Helmsley and Rievaulx Abbey, with an ancient church that pre-dates the Norman Conquest. Just opposite stood our objective, its proud wrought-iron sign announcing 'Ample Bosom' for anyone to see. Palpitating with expectation I drove into the farmyard. I don't really know what I thought I might see - perhaps a showroom dedicated to garments for maintaining the female chassis. Maybe stays (and cautions!), underpinning of all sorts and of epic proportions - brassieres you could use as a hammock and corsets you could camp out in; posters to make one blush and products and devices the purposes of which could only be dimly guessed at.

As it happened, the whole operation was efficient and enterprising, consisting of a few computer screens and desks in a converted barn, run by smart-suited ladies. It really was disappointing. I was just about to give up when my eye was caught by a garment fluttering gaily in the breeze on a washing line outside. It was one solitary brassiere - but what a brassiere! It was the size of a windsock - the sort usually seen next to the control tower at aerodromes. I felt gratified.

Chapter 19
Pubs and Ale

'When you have lost your inns
drown your empty selves, for you will
have lost the last of England' - Hilaire Belloc

One of the advantages of our accommodation was that it provided a list of recommended pubs in the area. This featured brief résumés of the type of establishment, style of cuisine, etc. plus a comment about the ambience. Entries would recommend this fish dish or that meat dish, along with the different beers. In my experience this is not a common phenomenon for self-catering establishments. Usually, they have leaflets for castles and candle-making and suchlike but in Yorkshire recommending pubs seems natural and normal.

Pubs are a way of life here and the standard of the beer has to be good, as the locals simply will not put up with a bad pint. A fairly cursory study of 'The Good Beer Guide' gives some idea of the sheer scale of the Yorkshire fondness for ale. It is not just the mass of entries for good pubs that impresses but the number of breweries located in the county. If you compare the figures with other counties you will see what I mean. For example, in the early 21st century there were six independent breweries in Cheshire, seven in Derbyshire, thirteen in Norfolk, seventeen in the whole of Wales put together and, astonishingly, ninety-six in Yorkshire!! The appetite for the substance is frankly stupendous. The brewing process is even depicted on the stained glass window of a church in York.

When you have your beer you need somewhere to drink it. It is miserable drinking on your own, especially in your own home, and that is where the pub comes into its own. The pub is a unique and special English invention, imitated in many countries but never quite as successfully. In foreign hands pubs either become drinking dens, where you wouldn't take your grandmother, or restaurants, which don't have the conviviality of the pub. As you drive across the dales the most frequent landmarks are pubs and churches. Every village has at least one of each and, like the hills they inhabit, the pub is a great social leveller (and I would hope that the church is too). Whether you are climbing a hill or drinking in a pub you are only the same as everyone else, you are no more or less important than the next guy; you can be a king or a pauper but you will get treated equally. Do you remember the TV footage of President Clinton popping into a pub in Oxford and shaking hands with a down-and-out at the bar? The pub is a wonderful institution.

Pub names fascinate me as well. Pub signs and names probably originated when some old ale-wife wanted to advertise the fact that her home brew was ready and for sale, so that she could earn a few extra pennies. Beer was sold to take away or to drink in a front room and all went well with this system until in the 1300s Richard II decided that taxing such ale houses was a spiffing way to raise revenue. It became a legal requirement to have a licence to sell alcohol in a 'public' house, and has been ever since. Pub signs became compulsory to help tax collectors identify the pubs. Interestingly, in medieval times it was illegal to spend more than a short time in a pub in any one day in order to stop the workforce getting drunk. Often there were notices pinned to the outside forbidding 'tippling'. I wonder how many were able to read them.

Pubs were often named after the coat of arms of the monarch, or after some local great man, such as 'The Red Lion', which was the sign of John of Gaunt, the founder of The House of Lancaster, and a common pub name throughout the Pennines (even the Yorkshire part!). Others are named after military campaigns such as 'The Saracen's Head', which goes back to the time of the Crusades. One of the oldest pubs in the country is 'Ye Olde Trip to Jerusalem' in Nottingham, which was a staging post for men on the way to fight for Christendom in the 12ᵗʰ century.

Then there are the idiosyncratic pub names based on a whole range of things. Perhaps the casement of a pub got changed and so it became known as 'The Case is Altered'; perhaps one of the locals visited a pub a bit too often, and through him it got the name 'Last in First Out'; a pub's cat ran away and then returned one day, hence 'The Cat's Back'. These are all genuine pub names, but how did they come by them? Well, picture the scene at a pub called say, 'The Duke of York'. The landlady is fond of the cat and there is much anguish and gnashing of teeth when one day it goes missing. The locals institute a search far and wide; posters are put up et cetera. The cat however, cannot be found. Cue much consternation, gossip and general interest until the topic fades with time. At some point in the future the cat suddenly and dramatically re-appears, jumping on the bar, purring and becoming the immediate focal point for the regulars. To a man they chorus "The cat's back!" and, lo and behold, you have enough impetus there and then to catapult the offending moggy to fame and immortality by renaming the pub in honour of its miraculous return. I think this romantic scenario perfectly illustrates the workings of a proper pub.

One that caught my eye on Ample Bosom's list was an entry at the very bottom that mentioned a pub in a village called Chop Gate. It simply said, 'No food but you have *got* to see it!' This intriguing comment set my antennae twitching so, early next morning, I rang up said establishment, and the conversation went something like this:

"Hello, is that the pub at Chop Gate?"

"Hang on (indecipherable), I'll just get him."

(Long pause, followed by further indecipherable mutterings, then footsteps) "Hello!"

"Hello, is that the pub?"

(Pause---suspiciously) "Yes."

"Oh good, err...I was wondering whether you were you open this lunch-time?"

(Aggrieved and indignant) "We're open all day!"

"Ah...do you do *any* food at all?"

"No."

"Err-r, do you allow dogs?"

"Yes."

"Good, thank you."

(Pause) "What time will you be coming then?"

"Pardon me?"

(Emphatic) "What time?"

"Oh (cough) about one o'clock."

"Right then," ('click', as receiver goes down).

This promised to be a bit of an escapade and I enthusiastically shared the phone call with Jane but her response was I thought, a little disappointing. Indeed, when we first dated I asked her if she would like to go for a drink. She replied that she didn't drink.

"Well," I said, "you can come and watch me!"

Chop Gate sounded great!

We set off briskly and the journey took us up country, past Rievaulx Abbey onto the B1257. It promised to be a perfect day, blue skies but not too warm, and we had the road to ourselves, apart from several hundred beautiful (though demented) pheasants, which ran across the lane, criss-crossing like single-minded commuters late for work. It was difficult to avoid them at anything over five miles per hour, particularly with the early morning sunlight streaming through the beautiful leaves of oak trees and silver birch. We wound down from Old Byland until suddenly, in a valley before us appeared the abbey, its soaring, skeletal arches just throwing off the early mists of the day. It was a haunting sight, but in a good way; a wholesome sort of haunting when you considered the years of toil of the faithful who had constructed it.

We couldn't help but stop and take a look and, as it happened, there was no-one else there. What a privilege to wander around this dream of the Middle Ages with only the cooing of the doves and the distant cackling of the wooded pheasants to break the silence. Was it as peaceful as this I wonder, back in the day when a novice Cistercian monk would hurry off to prayers at 5am? Or, would the problems of the human condition encroach even in this demi-paradise? Perhaps he was late, or ill and in pain. Perhaps he longed to see his family or an old flame, deserted now because of a higher calling? Jane jolted me out of this reverie, which was in danger of taking me on a downward spiral, by taking my arm and pointing out the sweep of the valley all around, in which the abbey nestled prettily.

"It reminds me a lot of the trollocks," she remarked, engagingly.

We paced on a while together whilst I filtered through the possible meanings of such a remark.

"You know," she continued, "that abbey in Scotland."

It transpired that she meant Kelso Abbey in the Trossachs, which we had once visited. To be fair, it is a valid comparison as both abbeys still have enough of the walls remaining, despite the ravages of time and Henry VIII, to imagine the lofty and ambitious footprint of the buildings. Rievaulx had been a powerful centre of learning, farming and industry in its prime, planting daughter establishments in both England and Scotland but alas, like so many human organisations, it had got into debt due to the grand design of its developments and ambitious plans for expansion. Maybe the glorification of Man took over from that of God!

'What about the beer'? I hear you imploring. 'You promised us ale'! I apologise to anyone thus exercised and, as we scurry out of the abbey and off to Chop Gate, trying to miss pheasants on the way, there is just time to pop in to another hostelry in the rather well-heeled town of Helmsley. There, as I ordered my pint of Black Sheep at the bar, I couldn't help but notice a chap next to me sipping whisky and dressed in plus-fours. We nodded and murmured at each other and soon struck up a conversation, as one should in a pub. It turned out that the guy was American and had flown over for the weekend, by private jet (!) from New York to York, to go grouse and pheasant shooting. He said that he had been doing this trip for many years in the hunting season, which accounted for the plus-fours I suppose. I speculated that he spent his leisure time jetting round the world taking advantage of various unfortunate creatures in their native habitats. I think I was talking to the last of 'the great, white hunters'. Perhaps, when after wild boar in Germany, he wore lederhosen. Or, maybe he dressed up as Captain Ahab to go whaling!

He told me how many pheasants he had shot that weekend, an impressive number, but I didn't want to disillusion him by telling him that I had probably run over more than that in the car.

We wished each other luck and soon after Jane and I were back on the road to Chop Gate, which gets its name from the Old Norse 'ceap' meaning 'pedlar'. There was not a lot happening in the village when we arrived, just before 1 pm. There were two pubs and a pub museum, which was run by The National Trust (only in Yorkshire!), but on inspection none of them exhibited any sign of life at all. We walked around the back of one establishment and suddenly I detected movement behind a very gloomy window. Emboldened I knocked on the dilapidated door and was greeted by a clattering noise, followed by shuffling and muffled muttering. The door creaked open to reveal an ancient, ancient lady. She was stooped and wizened, and wore a headscarf and apron, on which she wiped her hands. I couldn't help wondering if she had modelled for the 'old lady who lived in a shoe'. Recovering my composure I asked politely whether the pub might possibly be open. She did not reply directly but stared at me for a moment before shouting back over her shoulder,

"George, somebody wants the pub!"

Having said all she was apparently going to say this old 'gammer' turned and hobbled back into her kitchen, which looked as if it was being prepared for the arrival of Hansel and Gretel.

There was no time to dwell on this though as straightaway another aged nursery rhyme character tottered into view carrying what turned out to be an extremely large key, of the kind that locks dungeons; I assumed this to be George. He was obviously the crooked man who lived in a crooked house and, accordingly, he smiled a crooked smile and beckoned for us to enter. The enormous key unlocked a door on the front of the house and we were ushered into what I suppose used to be called a lounge pub or a farm pub.

These days it would be called a 'theme-pub', the theme in this case being 1960s transport café. There were a few old melamine-covered tables and plastic chairs, of the school canteen sort. On the floor was some scoured lino (you couldn't call it vinyl), and dingy net curtains covered the window looking out onto the road. To one side was a small bar at which George assumed the pose of landlord, after first striking a match to ignite a tatty calor gas heater. He looked slightly more comfortable installed behind the bar and beamed at us crookedly.

"What can I get you?" he asked.

I could imagine my wife answering, "Out of here!" so I quickly ordered some drinks and engaged George in conversation.

"How long have you worked here?" I queried, expecting a goodly period of time to be mentioned.

When he replied, "Eighty years," I nearly fell off my bar stool.

"Yes," he continued, "Man and boy. I started collecting glasses when I was eight and eventually became landlord."

"Are you a Free House?" I asked.

"Oh, yes," confirmed the old man. "Sometimes we get these pub companies ringing up offering this and that. They ask whether we have any entertainment here. I always reply yes – conversation." He chuckled.

In the end we had a good time with George, eventually deciding to leave before the rush! I reflected on what it must be like to spend all your life in one place. Were George and his wife any less happy and fulfilled for spending eighty-eight years in this beautiful area, without travelling abroad or even moving house? Had they led a less significant life, been a worse husband or wife, encountered fewer opportunities for doing good? I'm not sure - but I doubt it. Certainly they were keeping the art of conversation going and a sense of community, which has to be a good thing.

I don't know what the future holds for this splendid pub but I think that Hilaire Belloc would have approved of it.

Chapter 20
Dracula

*'But, strangest of all, the very instant
the shore was touched, an immense
dog sprang up on deck from below
and running forward jumped
from the bow on to the sand.
Making straight for the steep cliff,
where the churchyard hangs
over the laneway to the East
Pier…it disappeared in the darkness.'*

Bram Stoker wrote Dracula mainly in Whitby. He loved the place and was a frequent visitor, often staying at 'The Royal Hotel' on West Cliff. The view from the lounge looks out over the harbour towards East Cliff, where you can see St Mary's Church and Whitby Abbey. The east and west sides of Whitby are bisected by the harbour at the mouth of the River Esk, and the graveyard stands precariously close to the cliff edge, overlooking the end of the quay. It is one of the first things described in Stoker's novel and he was so impressed with the panorama that he made it the backdrop for his dark antagonist's arrival in England. The quote above describes the moment when the Count is shipwrecked off Whitby harbour and exits the stricken vessel in the form of a large dog.

Talk of vampires leads naturally to white necks, and speaking of white necks and suchlike, we had left 'Ample Bosom' and travelled east across the North York Moors to get to Whitby and the coast. This is a fun route to try in winter, when the snow is up to your armpits. It feels a bit like travelling across the surface of the moon, with the sense that if you break down they will probably never discover your frozen body, with your frozen fingers poised over your mobile phone.

In days of yore, large stone monuments were erected as way-markers for packhorse travellers, wayward monks and the like. One or two of them remain, such as 'Old Ralph's Cross' and 'Young Ralph's Cross', which stand close by the pretty village of Hutton-le-Hole. These days the 'Lyke Wake Walk' crosses the moors near here which is said to be based on a story of the soul's journey through the underworld; in the snow this would seem to be appropriate.

When it eventually comes, the coast is a surprise. For almost an hour you drive through flat-topped moorland and then, suddenly, Whitby Abbey and the east coast cliff tops appear, diving dramatically into the sea. It makes you want to brake hard, open-mouthed, to take in the enormity of this serendipitous change of scenery. The abbey and cliffs at first obscure the town of Whitby, which snuggles cosily on either side of the harbour. The streets are so precipitous that the houses appear to tumble on top of one another down to the sea.

Whitby is a place of great beauty and character, where Yorkshire and all that it stands for meets the mighty ocean; an irresistible force meets an immovable object! The outskirts of the town are really quite posh, with some elegant Victorian hotels and parks and (always) those lovely views. The road descends steeply and quickly into the centre where there is a mishmash of narrow streets, reflecting Whitby's long and colourful past.

There are fishermen's cottages here, as you might expect, but also there are the quaint little homes of those who were once employed in mining and quarrying. An extraordinary variety of minerals were extracted from the hills round here including ironstone, sandstone, jet, whinstone, clay, limestone, coal, alum, potash and salt. It is a wonder that there is any land at all left hereabouts as these minerals have been exported all over the world, but the mines and quarries are gone now leaving only the fishing industry still in evidence.

The cottages spill onto the quayside, which travels up both sides of the harbour. East and west are connected by an impressive Victorian swing bridge that is fun to watch in action. An old chap wanders out from a little hut and imperiously stops the traffic with a wave of his hand. He then sweeps pedestrians off the bridge, engaging in some Yorkshire banter the while. At his signal the bridge starts to swing open, imperceptibly at first, and completely silent - a tribute to Victorian engineering. After several minutes the mighty structure is at ninety degrees to its normal position and everyone watches, wonderingly, as some tiny ketch sails rather sheepishly through the opening. The whole procedure is then reversed, with lots more banter.

On the water there is a brisk commerce of boats, some for fishing, but mostly pleasure craft. If you want you can take a trip round the harbour on a scaled-down version of Captain Cook's ship, the 'Endeavour', to look at the lighthouse and the dramatic coastline. Captain James Cook is probably Whitby's most august son. He was born nearby in 1728 and though he came from a poor family, with ten brothers and sisters, he was a lad of ability and ambition, who ended up as a captain in the Royal Navy. He showed such promise that he was commissioned to survey the Southern Ocean, to ascertain whether there might be a large land mass 'down under' as was suspected.

It is a misconception that Cook discovered Australia but he did discover New Zealand in 1769 (although technically it was a cabin boy called Nicholas Young who spotted land first). Tasman had observed it 100 years before but, crucially, he did not set foot on shore.

Cook's achievements were many. He went on to discover Hawaii and other Pacific islands, as well as charting the Bering Strait. Although he was not the first to Australia, he did explore the eastern seaboard and named Botany Bay. He remains so famous in Australia that in 1934 an Australian businessman paid to have the little cottage that Cook had grown up in dismantled and shipped to Melbourne, where it was re-erected in a park, and where it remains to this day.

Cook was killed in 1779 in Hawaii, after a dispute with local tribes about the theft of one of his boats. Cook was stabbed on the beach as he confronted tribal chiefs, who later took out his heart, roasted it and ate it. Apparently it was because he was a religious icon to them, and they always ate religious icons!

Some of this information can be heard being piped through the PA system of the miniature version of Cook's ship during its trips round Whitby harbour. They also pipe through sea shanties and encourage people to join in. Unhappily, the lyrics of most of them are not very edifying, dealing as they do with the dubious activities of men cooped up together for months on end on ships, but the jolly tourists seem unaware of this fact and sing along enthusiastically.

As you walk up the quay nearly every property seems to be a pub or a fish and chip shop. The beer is good (naturally), but the fish and chips are superlative - an art form in batter. Be prepared to queue for over two hours though at some of the more famous 'chippies'. Most other commercial premises are cake shops or sweet shops, but there is one health food shop that stands, rather forlornly, on the east side of the swing bridge. Unfortunately, it does not appear to do the same brisk trade enjoyed by the other establishments. Indeed there are so many fryeries, bakers and confectioners that you might expect the population to be rolling around like Mr Wobbly Man in 'Noddy' – but they don't particularly. They must stay fit walking up and down the hills, which cover every bit of Whitby.

If you look up from practically any point in the town then you cannot fail to notice St Mary's Church and the ruins of Whitby Abbey. The abbey looms so atmospherically, crying out for investigation and therefore, after we had unloaded our gear at our lodgings, we set off to ascend the steep and winding steps that take you up from the quay. You need to be fairly energetic to attempt this as there are 199 of them. At various points you meet wheezing, red-faced tourists, collapsed on one of the helpfully sited benches, placed to take best advantage of the view and convenient for the local St John's Ambulance service.

St Mary's church can be found near the top and we decided to have a look round, if for no better reason than to break up the climb. The graveyard, which so impressed Bram Stoker, has many headstones with inscriptions that bear tribute to the fishermen, sailors and passengers who have lost their lives at sea over the years, and also of some of the lifeboatmen who tried to rescue them. Thankfully, many more lives were saved than lost due to their bravery.

One dark night, in the middle of winter in 1881, a small schooner ran aground off Robin Hood's Bay, six miles from Whitby. They tried to launch the Whitby lifeboat but the weather was too bad. Snow mixed with spume from the wind-whipped sea and the waves were enormous. Unbelievably, the crew of the lifeboat dragged it overland for six miles to the site of the disaster, aided by local people. What's worse, the snow lay thick on the ground and had to be shovelled out of the way en route. When they reached the shores of Robin Hood's Bay the crew dropped their shovels, picked up their oars, rowed out to the stricken vessel and managed to rescue the entire crew!

Now that shows courage and endurance, does it not?

Other rescues have been equally brave, including that of the 'Rohilla', a passenger ship from Dublin, wrecked off Saltwick in 1914. Although dozens sadly died hundreds were saved, including the ship's cat and a certain Mary Roberts, who had survived the sinking of the 'Titanic' two years earlier. I imagine that after this episode she probably stayed at home a lot more.

As we know, the graveyard is the site of first landfall for Stoker's Dracula. The town has a thriving industry based on the novel and you can watch

Dracula films, listen to Dracula music, follow a Dracula trail and, no doubt, buy Dracula fish and chips, with little cocktail sticks as fangs! Many visitors are drawn here because of the toothy Transylvanian and there are endless numbers of look-alikes wandering around but, if I am honest, I found the fixation on matters dark and deathly a little oppressive.

St Mary's Church is definitely the most eccentric I have ever been in. The porch and vestibule look pretty similar to many ancient churches, excepting that the bell ropes (and ringers) are visible to the left as you walk in. There would be nothing to stop one wandering casually over and yanking on a bell rope, thereby starting a panic in the town (this being the warning against Viking invaders or some such).

As you enter the main body of the church there is a sign hinting that failure to make a donation might result in grave consequences, in the same way that the criminal underworld might demand protection money – with menaces. Suitably chastened we stepped inside, and were at once struck by the layout of the pews in the nave. They do not face in one direction to the front but they are a series of interconnected boxes, of varying size, each side of every box having a form or settle in front of it. This means that each box pew could seat up to fifteen people, who would all be facing one another, like passengers on the Underground. Some pews were labelled for the use of certain privileged families and others were 'for the use of strangers'; some others were for church-wardens and some, curiously, for 'the use of church maids'.

Above the box pews are galleried seats, on four sides, in the style of an 18th century Methodist church. They all look down on a pulpit that must have come straight out of the imagination of Heath Robinson, or even Salvador Dali. It is three-tiered, like a wedding cake, with finials and fluting and, at the top, a tester and a gigantic ear trumpet. It soars to an enormous height, narrowing sharply as it teeters and totters to a pinnacle or crown.

Directly beneath this strange spire there are windows looking out in every direction, and beneath them comfortable sofas or day beds are positioned, presumably to allow two or three members of the clergy to recline at ease whilst regaling the congregation. The ear trumpet was installed over one hundred years ago because the vicar at that time was profoundly deaf and couldn't hear the responses without amplification. It was so bizarre that I half expected the White Rabbit to come tottering down its narrow steps at any moment.

Next to this extraordinary structure stands an immense, ancient coke-burner, and with it a large bucket of coke and a shovel for feeding the monstrous belly of the stove. It is inscribed with the name of a 19th century Birmingham ironworks and it has a great stove-pipe that travels up the full height of the church, before disappearing through the ceiling.

On the other side of the pulpit is an 18ᵗʰ century wooden gallery that covers up most of the chancel. It is painted gaudily, at odds with the oak panelling round about, and which looks more in keeping with a fairground than a church. It was built without permission by the local lord of the manor, Lord Cholmley, in order to seat his family away from the masses. The church authorities were outraged and fined him £2,000 (a huge sum at the time) and ordered him to remove it. The local parish council however simply pocketed the money and allowed the gallery to remain. Do things of questionable taste improve with age? I am not sure - you'll have to ask my wife! It still looked a bit tacky to me.

Eccentricity continued in the display of a fairly random collection of dolls underneath the gallery, some old and some new, without much explanation given as to why they were there. I understand that this is where James Cook worshipped and I can sympathise therefore with his desire to explore foreign shores.

We left shortly after this, just as one of the wardens was leaning perilously over the gallery to adjust the wall clock that was fixed to it.

"She's the only one as can reach it," beamed another warden as we walked past, back through the nave into the vestibule.

"There's a funeral at 12 o'clock," she confided.

This obviously explained the presence of the bell-ringers (or campanologists) and they seemed to be getting ready to ring (or camp?) just as we stepped out into the sunlight. I expected some sombre tolling to begin but no, as we were leaving the graveyard for the nearby abbey joy bells broke out in a rapturous peel that could have been heard all over Whitby. I do not understand Yorkshire folk. Maybe the dearly departed had not been very popular.

The abbey is practically next to the church, perched on the edge of the cliffs that fall away into the North Sea. The view is spectacular and the wind bracing! Whether it was the view, the wind, or the fact that the abbey is visible for miles, I am not certain why this particular site was chosen. I suppose the nearby harbour was a useful asset for transporting stone for building, or for facilitating the ebb and flow of ecclesiastical persons. It was founded by Hilda in 657AD, a lady of formidable ability and virtuous character. Hilda had connections to the Northumbrian royal family and played a part in getting the king to host a synod at Whitby to debate 'correct' church practice. As usual people had fallen out over methods of worship, some favouring the Celtic model and others the Roman model. It was a very distinguished gathering, including King Oswiu and Bishop Colman of Northumbria, who were of the Celtic persuasion, and Queen Eanflaed and Bishop Wilfrid, from Kent, who were in the Roman camp. The Roman arguments won the day at what became known as the Synod of Whitby and this formed the basis for the spread of the Catholic faith throughout England. The Celtic monks who were not able to accept this decision moved out of

Whitby to Iona and then to Ireland. This was to be another North/South divide!

It is said that seabirds flying past the abbey dip their wings in salute to the memory of Hilda and that ammonite fossils on the beach below are, in fact, the remains of snakes that the abbess turned into stone when they plagued the abbey. There is still a Priory called St Hilda's at nearby Sneaton Castle, inhabited by nuns of the splendid 'Order of the Holy Paraclete'.

After Hilda's death in 680 not much more is heard of the abbey until its destruction by the Vikings in 867. There is one little snippet though from the historian the Venerable Bede who bemoans the fact that the abbey became a place of licentiousness and drunkenness after the good Abbess had passed on.

We had a good look round the abbey and its treasures, the only slight problem being that if you wear the recommended audio-link headsets then you are in danger of bumping into other people wandering around similarly equipped, as everyone is concentrating so intently on trying to find the bit of the abbey being described at that moment. I never seemed to be in the right place at the right time. The machine would be intoning things like:

"If you look to your left you will notice the 7th century arch",

whereas, in fact, when I looked to the left I could only see the toilets.

This was also the site of the manor house belonging to the Cholmleys (of church gallery notoriety) who had bought the land when the abbey was dissolved. In my head I had been confusing them with the Cholmondeley family, whose seat is at Cholmondeley Castle near Chester. Both names are pronounced 'Chumly' so you could excuse the WWI correspondent of The Yorkshire Post, Horatio Bottomley, who had been sent to Cholmondeley ('Chumly') Castle to do a comparison between the two famous families. He kept wanting to pronounce the Cheshire name as 'Chol-mon-del-ey'. The story goes that Horatio Bottomley arrived at Cholmondeley Castle and enquired of the butler if he could see Lord Chol-mon-del-ey. The butler looked down his nose at Bottomley and replied snootily,

"It's pronounced 'Chumly', sir."

"Well," responded our hack, full of Yorkshire pride, "tell him Horatio Bumley has come to see him!"

We walked back down the one hundred and ninety-nine steps, which is not good for the knees, and crossed back over the swing bridge to our lodgings. Below us the scaled-down 'Endeavour' was just sailing by, her happy passengers cheerfully carolling a song that revolved mostly around a practice banned in the vast majority of US states. People were wandering along the quayside eating fish and chips and the pubs were doing a roaring trade. I reflected benignly on this vibrant little place. Long may it remain as it is - the most easterly outpost of the Yorkshire Pennines.

We had dinner at a pub near the foot of the abbey steps called 'The Black Horse'. This pub has one of the oldest unchanged bars in England, and probably some of the oldest unchanged customers. A group of pensioners from Middlesbrough were already installed when we arrived, complaining happily about the price of the beer.

"You may complain," retorted the landlady, "but you're on your third round and you're still here!"

The pub serves the usual local beer, 'Captain Cook Ale', and, like all pubs, smoking is banned. They have got round this ban in an unusual way - by promoting snuff! Behind the bar was a large selection of the substance with helpful tasting notes (smelling notes?). I expected to see people snorting away in dark corners, sneezing extravagantly into stained handkerchiefs and leaving brown stains from their nostrils, but all seemed orderly and hygienic.

Thus reassured we went for the food. Just in front of the bar there was a hotplate with a small cauldron on it containing copious amounts of hotpot. The idea was that you paid £4.95 and then you ladled as much as you liked into a bowl and helped yourself to bread and butter. This was the only hot meal being served at lunchtime, which harks back to the traditional idea of pub fare, a system most often found nowadays in rural French cafes. It was delicious and nutritious, especially after braving the gales at the abbey.

After dinner we wandered around the town. I wanted to find a pub called 'First In Last Out', which we did eventually, after several false starts. I must have overdone the walking because next day my back started to give me some 'jip' and I had to rest at our lodgings. We were staying at the appropriately named 'Lancaster House', which actually belongs to my cousin (if you mention my name then I'm sure you could get a deal!). Sunk in an armchair, feeling gloomy, I looked out of the window at the seagulls. They seemed particularly large and bold. They called incessantly and loudly as they wheeled overhead or wandered up and down the narrow lane, and they didn't stop until nearly midnight. I noticed that every morning a little old lady came out of her house to feed them and this probably emboldened them to think of the area as their own. Eventually I contemplated murder.

Just down the lane was the tiniest Indian restaurant I have ever seen. It had only three tables and was run by a jolly chap who originally came from Bradford but who had lived in Whitby for a number of years. I could just about stagger down there for a curry, where we chatted genially about Yorkshire and why we both loved it. I mention this because of a strange train of thought I had when confined to my sickbed. I started to wonder when curry had first appeared in England, and determined to do a little research on the matter. For the answer to this question we must move further north, to the Roman wall!

Chapter 21
Vindaloo-landa

'(missimus tibi) subligariorum duo (we have sent you two pairs of underpants)'
-fragment of a Roman writing tablet discovered at Vindolanda, by Hadrian's Wall

Nobody really knows what happened to the Ninth Legion of the Roman Army - the records don't agree. Some say it was massacred on the Rhine, and some say it was decimated fighting in the Eastern Empire, but most academics seem to think it was lost trying to subdue the war-like tribes of Northern England. Actually it just vanished - all 6,000 men - probably in Yorkshire. It was last seen in York in 108 AD and shortly after leaving on patrol it disappeared, never to return. The natives were definitely restless in the North.

There have been various works of fiction based on this mysterious legion, notably Rosemary Sutcliff's 'The Eagle of the Ninth', a novel written in 1954. Interestingly, the hero of the story is a Roman and the 'good guys' are the Roman army. The Northerners are depicted as primitive, treacherous cut-throats, rather like Red Indians used to be portrayed in the old Westerns. A Hollywood blockbuster was made in 2011 called simply 'The Eagle', and once again it is the Romans with whom we are meant to identify. I can't think of one other film in which the Romans are the 'goodies'. From 'Anthony and Cleopatra', through 'Spartacus', 'The Robe', and 'Ben Hur', and on to 'Gladiator', they are always bad. So why the sudden change? There must even be a retrospective North/South divide!

The Emperor Hadrian came over to try and solve the problem in 122 AD and left muttering,

"The Britons could not be kept under Roman control."

He did build a wall though and it is there that we are now heading. To get to Hadrian's Wall we have to travel northwest of Whitby, just tiptoeing round the outskirts of Geordie-land. The origin of the word 'Geordie' is obscure but it may be a reference to their support for King George II of England, as opposed to King James II of Scotland, during the Jacobite rebellion in 1745. Suffice to say it can refer both to the dialect and people of this region.

Geordie has been voted England's favourite accent in poll after poll and I tend to agree that there is something appealing about it. It can be a hard one to imitate, and one voice coach advises starting with the days of the week. If you pronounce the sound '-ay' as '-ear' then you might just have found a way in to this elusive accent. Thus: 'Mond-ear', 'Tuesd-ear', 'Wednesd-ear', and so on.

The onset of Geordie starts quite suddenly, a bit like Scouse. If you cross a particular road in St Helens you go from the rich, flat deep tones of Lancashire to the fast, high-pitched ones of Liverpool. In the Northeast it is the same. Somewhere about Middlesborough sonorous Yorkshire turns into inquisitive Geordie with that rising inflection as you approach the end of a sentence. It is interesting to think that when you hear Geordie you are probably closer to the sound of Old English than anywhere else in the country.

Something else that Merseyside and Tyneside have in common is a good sense of humour. Take this joke about Geordie pronunciation; to understand it you need to know that in Geordie the word 'work' is pronounced 'walk' and the word 'walk' is pronounced 'wark'.

A Geordie has an operation on his leg and afterwards his surgeon comes on to the ward to see him.

"You mustn't walk for two weeks," says the surgeon.

"Walk!" exclaimed the man, "I can't even wark!"

Then there is the story of old Jim and his wife Alice, who were woken in the night by the sound of German bombers flying over the docks of Tyneside during the Second World War. Jim scrambled for the air-raid shelter in the garden but his wife lagged behind.

"Come on lass," urged Jim. "What are you waiting for?"

"I'm looking for my teeth," replied Alice.

"Eeh, Pet!" said Jim, "They're dropping bombs, not pork pies!"

From Whitby we made for Durham, which at one time was the capital of Deira, a kingdom that included present day Tyneside, Northumberland, Durham, Yorkshire, parts of Lancashire and the east coast of Scotland – as far as The Firth of Forth. In the 7th century Deira was a realm of international importance, an ecclesiastical centre, and a beacon of learning and culture throughout Europe. It produced the Venerable Bede, who was probably the first great 'English' historian and writer. Literature also flourished in the person of Caedmon the poet, who had been 'discovered' by Hilda, at Whitby Abbey. It is said that the poetry of Caedmon is more understandable if you are familiar with Geordie dialect.

The Vikings put a stop to all this by invading and laying waste to the country, including its abbeys like Lindisfarne, which was devastated in 793 AD. The monks had to abandon it and carried the bones of its founder, St Cuthbert, to the relative safety of Durham. In the 12th century Durham was known as 'The Land of the Prince Bishops', a title it kept until the middle of the 19th century. Jane asked if this was a Bishopric but I couldn't say. It was the centre of what remained of the quasi-independent state of the North of England. In the 1300s the condition of England was described by one commentator like this,

'There are two Kings in England namely The Lord King of England, wearing a crown in sign of his regality, and The Lord Bishop of Durham wearing a mitre in place of a crown, in sign of his regality in the diocese of Durham'.

This arrangement may well have given rise to the pub name 'The Crown and Mitre'.

Although William the Conqueror had taken most of England in 1066, the north of the country was not properly under control (some might say that it still isn't). He quickly realised that to protect the south from attack, from alliances of Vikings, Saxons and Scots, he had to secure friendship with Northumbria. This went well up to the point where 700 of William's negotiating team were murdered, in Durham, in 1069. He was not best pleased with this turn of events and marched north with his army to lay waste to the whole of the North of England. This infamous episode came to be known as 'The Harrying (or 'harrowing') of the North'. William aimed to slaughter the entire population from the Humber to the Tees and, after he had slaughtered, he burned the land and then salted it, so that it could not grow crops. What was left of the population was reduced first to eating cats and dogs and then each other. Over 100,000 are thought to have died of starvation. At that time it certainly was 'grim up north'.

William installed his own 'yes man' in Durham but The North continued to rebel from time to time. Durham still retains an air of power and independence to my mind. This is evidenced in the cathedral's description of itself as 'The most important Norman cathedral in the country, if not in Europe'.

The North will rise again!

Much has been written about the beauty of the cathedral, standing as it does on a hilly island above the River Wear. It looks impressive without being over-bearing, a Romanesque masterpiece. The only problem is that it has to be approached by a slog up a big hill from the car park. This might necessitate a stop at 'The Shakespeare Inn', which I always looked forward to on a visit to Durham. It can be found just before you reach the cathedral square. Last time I imbibed here the 'Shakespeare' had been a proper pub. It was not really big on food; it had a stone floor and a gleaming wood panelled bar. It also had a snug with a ghost!

The revisit proved to be a huge disappointment. Dribbling in anticipation I flung open the door only to be confronted by a wine bar. The snug had been knocked through to make one gigantic space, and everything was brilliant white. In fact they had painted the character out of the whole place and made it bland and artificial. This is disgraceful. When are we going to start cherishing our pub heritage? What will the ghost think?

Stumbling out in shock and disgust Jane and I made for the cathedral. Perhaps they had knocked that through as well, and painted it white. Approaching the door though it seemed to be just as I had remembered it. The door of Durham Cathedral must be the most impressive I have seen. Like many similar places it has enormous, iron-studded double doors, but what makes Durham's unique is the amazing medieval door knocker. It is formed in brass, in the shape of the head of an enormous lion, which is also the symbol of the city. People used to beg for sanctuary in the cathedral by knocking on the door but, as far as we know, never in its 900 year history has anyone tried to steal the knocker. That is until 2010, when some twerp scaled the gates of the square and then tried to wrench it off the door. Fortunately the original was removed for safe keeping in 1980, so if they had succeeded in removing it they would only have been getting a replica. They were probably going to melt it down for scrap!

The interior has all the usual awe-inspiring features of such places and one can marvel at the free-standing Lady Chapel with its intricately carved stone arcades, but what made it for me was the tomb of St Cuthbert. Here indeed you have the bones of a great pillar of the early church in England. Cuthbert's tomb can be found at the south door of the Feretory. I know this sounds like it might be the ferret equivalent of a rabbit warren but it just means a place in a church where relics are kept. The great saint rests here now but he has moved about a bit in his time. Originally buried on Lindisfarne, he was exhumed by his fellow monks when the Vikings invaded and carried round Northumbria for eleven years, before finally ending up in Durham. It was said that he could still do miracles from the grave and his tomb became a shrine and a place of pilgrimage. I wished he could do something about 'The Shakespeare Inn'. Looking at the bored people wandering past or squatting on Cuthbert's tomb, I think I should be ready to dig him up and carry him away again.

Durham University was founded in 1832, although the teaching and learning of theology and history had probably been going on in the city since the time of Bede. It was the first university to be established in England for six hundred years, largely because Oxford and Cambridge guarded their unique position jealously. Although pushed for by the Church, Durham probably received its university status because of the support given by Earl Grey of Howick and Chillingham. His family seat was close to Durham and also he happened to be Prime Minister at the time.

I have to confess that I was bored with culture by now, Cuthbert not withstanding, and I left Jane to examine every last nook and cranny of Durham's heritage whilst I went scouring the charity shops. Jane accuses me of being only interested in charity shops and breweries when we are on holiday but in truth I am driven to this by her obsessive interest in historical buildings. I am not saying that I don't find such places of interest but normally half an hour is enough for me before I start getting itchy feet. Jane on the other hand takes an archaeological brush and a microscope on such visits. If there is a guide she will latch on to them like the most enthusiastic teacher's pet and hang on their every word, asking multitudinous questions about anything from the *trompe l'oeil* to the lord's underpants. On one occasion, whilst visiting Newbury Priory in North Yorkshire, she even buttonholed the guide on his coffee break and continued to bombard him with questions, demanding a response both encyclopaedic and erudite.

A little further north from Durham on the coast of Northumberland is Bamburgh, dominated by its huge castle standing on a promontory overlooking the beach. Here I was in for a night of more disappointment because our hotel didn't have real ale on tap. The barman looked astonished when I walked out of the bar, having failed to take him up on his offer of some fizzy cardboard, masquerading as lager.

Unusually for us this was quite a posh hotel, the sort where they arrange your nightwear decoratively on your pillow. This was fine for Jane who always wears elegant outfits in the boudoir. I, on the other hand, tend to cut up and rip the elasticated waistband on my boxer shorts because I hate to have my somewhat extensive stomach restricted. As a result they look shamefully scruffy and more suited for cleaning the floor. When we returned from our day out in Bamburgh I discovered that some poor chambermaid had tried to arrange my boxers artistically. The result was as if Picasso had been given a pile of tripe to work with!

We had booked to stay for a couple of nights in Bamburgh and I determined that I would enter into the spirit of this wild and woolly place by swimming in the North Sea. It was an impulsive decision. I looked at the magnificent castle, standing proudly above the beach, and imagined what it would have been like to be a Viking, landing here centuries ago. A craftier part of me wanted to prove to Jane that we had not missed out by choosing to holiday in the Pennines rather than Spain, and that the North Sea was as benign as the Mediterranean. Nevertheless, feeling my roots keenly I chucked my clothes to the ground and dived into the roaring surf. If I said it was mind-numbingly cold that would be an understatement. I did manage it, but when I walked out of the sea a little girl nearby asked,

"Mummy, why has that man turned blue?"

In ancient times Bamburgh Castle was a centre of power for the Kings of Northumbria, and possibly the site where Christianity was first preached in the North of England. The third King of Northumbria to profess Christianity was Oswald, who encouraged the foundation of monasteries, including one on Lindisfarne or 'Holy Island', in 634 AD.

Lindisfarne represents the very last fling of the Pennines as they crash into the sea at their northerly extreme. It is a lovely and interesting place and has featured in numerous films and TV programmes. To get there you have to wait for low tide and then you can drive across the causeway. You *have* to visit the island when you are up here and I looked forward to some solitude, meditation and rumination, walking around the abbey and its grounds. What I hadn't expected was to meet tens of thousands of other pilgrims, all looking for the same thing. It was more like Piccadilly Circus!

The trick is to stay the night, after the tourists have gone home and the tide has rolled in. This offers the opportunity to stay in one of the great pubs and also to join the locals watching the tourists leave. They allegedly run a book on which cars will try to make it back to the mainland when the sea is covering the causeway. It makes for great sport but, not wanting to genuinely endanger life, they have built a shed on stilts halfway along the causeway, so that if someone is overtaken by the incoming tide they can scamper up the ladder to safety. They call it 'The Nincompoop Box'.

A friend of mine, who works in television, was doing a religious broadcast from Lindisfarne. A farmer was driving his tractor up and down a field in the background and it made such a noise that the director went over and asked him if he wouldn't mind stopping for ten minutes. The farmer agreed, as long as they gave him £100. Without batting an eye the director took the cash from his wallet and gave it to the farmer, to allow them to continue with 'Songs of Praise', or whatever it was. What an uneasy mix of God and Mammon on 'Holy Island'.

Just down the coast from Lindisfarne and Bamburgh is the little town of Seahouses, where you can take a boat to the Farne Islands to look at birds. Sure, birds are great, but our latest trip to Seahouses remains memorable to me because of the Public Conveniences on the sea front. You have to buy a ticket to get in, which at twenty pence does not seem particularly cheap! I needed to go though so I bought my ticket and was obtaining relief in the usual manner when I happened to glance at the ticket, still in my hand. It announced its credentials as originating from the local council but underneath it continued in official and portentous tones, 'Please retain for inspection during use!'. I risked a nervous glance over my shoulder.

The interior of Northumberland is largely empty. Along with South Shropshire it is the least populated area of England. Here at last you can get away from the madding crowd. You can actually start to feel a sense of remoteness as you drive around inland, which is rare for England. Kielder Forest is very remote and I was surprised to find a pub right in the middle. I was even more surprised (or was I?) to find that the landlord was from Australia.

"I'd never even heard of Northumberland before I came here," he confided to me, somewhat ruefully I thought.

After a spending some time in this region you begin to notice the light. Something wonderful happens to light as you head north of Yorkshire. It becomes cool, clear and clean and it invests the natural world with brightness and vitality. The big skies, diverse landscapes and seascapes provide great backdrops for the immense numbers of migrating birds that cross Northumberland. Many artists have understood this, including Salford born L.S. Lowry, who painted more than thirty seascapes and buildings around Berwick-on-Tweed. Normally associated with industrial scenes the Northumbrian paintings provide an interesting contrast to his usual chimney-littered skylines.

Lowry met a chap called Norman Cornish in Newcastle Art Gallery and they became friends. Now in his nineties, Norman is probably the last surviving contemporary of that group known as 'The Pitmen Painters', so depicted in Lee Hall's play. They came mostly from Ashington in Northumberland and they were miners who had studied art at night school. Norman doesn't think that Hall's play does the men justice by portraying them as 'entertaining clowns'. He describes them as intelligent men who wanted to paint, but who were forced by circumstances to be coal miners. The work of this group was the first exhibition of western art to be featured in China at the end of the Cultural Revolution in 1984.

Norman's paintings are of the sights and daily life of Spennymoor in County Durham, and many of them portray the mobile fish and chip wagons that used to serve the local communities. I can remember my father talking about the 'pie and peas' man who used to push his barrow round Brighouse before the war. Typically, the most precious memory my father could recall of this interesting piece of folk history was that the 'pie and peas' man used to suffer from awful flatulence when he bent over to ladle out the mushy peas, having indulged too liberally of his own fare.

Inland from Bamburgh is Chillingham Castle, which has been in the gift of the Earls Grey since time immemorial. The Earls Grey are most memorable for two things. The first is the part played by the 2nd Earl Grey in the foundation of Durham University, and the second is giving their name and title to Earl Grey tea. Various legends have sprung up regarding the origins of this blend, which has the unusual ingredient of bergamot, a citrus fruit grown commercially in Italy. Some stories tell of the good deeds of the 2nd Earl Grey in China in 1803, as a sort of diplomatic super-hero. A grateful Chinese merchant is supposed to have passed on the secret tea recipe for services rendered. Others say that it was discovered by the 2nd Earl's wife in Italy and who served it to guests when her husband was Prime Minister in the 1830s. Whatever the truth, 'Earl

Grey Tea' proved to be a great success, and to this day still graces the tables of proper 'toffs'.

The drive of Chillingham Castle is long, and punctuated by wild cows. They are wild in both senses of the word. They are called 'the last wild cattle in the world', descendants of the bovines that roamed the forests of the Ancient Britons, and they are not found anywhere else. They have shaggy white coats and very long horns; this is where the other sense of wild comes in. You see, the beasts are not very friendly and should not be approached in any circumstances, except under the supervision of a keeper. We drove past the steaming belligerents a little nervously on the way in, setting the tone for what followed.

'Chilling'-ham Castle is a very apt name for the place, which is not part of the National Trust but is privately owned. One advantage this brings is that it is all very relaxed. You don't get a lot of uniformed attendants telling you exactly where you can go and where you can't. There are some roped-off areas but they are few and far between and pretty random. There are large parts that haven't been gentrified or renovated and this does help to instil a sense of the ancient nature of the castle. However, it doesn't mean that you might suddenly come across a big hole in the floor, or be alarmed by the imminent collapse of some buttress or battlement.

One of the featured attractions is a torture chamber. It looks a bit like 'The Haunted House' at Alton Towers, except that it is for real. It is sited in the dungeons of the castle with one tiny arrow-slit of a window to illuminate the instruments of torture. Here you may wander around and marvel at the rack, or the Iron Maiden, or perhaps amuse yourself by applying the thumb-screw to one of your loved ones. The Iron Maiden is a type of sarcophagus, intended to accommodate a person. You may step into it and have your photo taken, but don't close the lid - it has six-inch spikes attached to it!

Were all these horrible objects original or had they been collected over the years, like some more brutal equivalent of philately? Certainly, the chamber has been used as a prison in the past because you can still see etchings carved on the walls by former inmates, counting off the days. Disturbingly, if you lift the trapdoor in the centre of the room the very genuine skeleton of a child can be found at the bottom of a well.

Then there are the ghosts! Reputedly, there are dozens of them at Chillingham. It is supposed to be one of the most haunted places in Britain. You have the Blue Boy, who is the ghost of a child incarcerated in a wall. There is Wandering Mary, who gets about a bit, the White Pantry Ghost and the Dying Officer. In fact there are very few parts of the castle that don't have a ghost or two. You would be tripping over them if they had any substance!

The best has to be the Ghosts of War. This visitation was recorded by Lady Tankerville, who lived in the castle in the 1920s. She claims she witnessed an entire battle, with royal figures striding along the battlements, kneeling nuns, knights and hundreds of Scotsmen.

I don't know where you stand on the subject of unquiet spirits but if anywhere has got them it has to be this place. When you learn that children have been tortured and killed here and that there have been many well-recorded executions then it becomes more understandable. Some victims were decapitated and had their heads stuck on the top of the castle gates. Some were less fortunate and were hanged drawn and quartered, which means basically that they were turned into sausage-meat before their very own eyes!

The current incumbent of Chillingham, Sir Humphrey Wakefield Bt., chucklingly comments of the ghosts,

"They are part of our lives...and we are part of theirs."

That's as maybe, but I wouldn't stay in one of the self-catering apartments here for love nor money.

From Chillingham we wend our way east and slightly south, through Northumberland National Park to Hadrian's Wall. Built on the orders of the Roman Emperor Hadrian in 122 AD it stretches from Bowness on the Solway Firth in the west, 73 miles to Wallsend in the east, across the narrowest part of England. The wall is 9ft 7inches wide and 16-20 ft high, and every mile it has a Milecastle - a little guardhouse or keep, originally manned by soldiers.

People tend to think that the wall is on the Scottish/English border and designed to keep out the warring Picts, but this is not strictly the case. In the first place the bulk of the wall is more than 60 miles south of the Scottish border, particularly in the east. It is quite possible that it acted just as often as the Roman equivalent of the Inland Revenue, a place to collect taxes from traders.

The Roman town of Vindolanda stood halfway along Hadrian's Wall, not far from modern day Hexham. It acted as a fort and trading post and guarded the main road that ran south of the wall along its whole length. Recent archaeological digs have discovered all sorts of interesting artefacts, including a pile of wooden tablets on which inventories and invoices had been etched. This suggests that there was a whole lot of trading going on and traffic from both sides of the wall passing through; like some sort of cross between 'Checkpoint Charlie' and Sainsbury's.

Of course, the wall was also a massive status symbol, meant to scare and overawe the natives so that they would not be as keen to start any trouble. It must have looked hugely impressive, up to 20ft high and over 70 miles long, bristling with Roman legionaries. Possibly, it had a type of whitewash covering it, which must have made it appear both alien and insuperable.

New artefacts are being unearthed at Vindolanda on a daily basis. It is an exciting place to wander round because so much of it is complete, such as the religious shrines and temples. They give one some sense of what the Roman religion was all about. Many of the decorations and totems are not unlike those to be found in Christian churches. The walls and floors have warm and comforting colours and there are mosaics, icons and stained glass. There are little stations with amphora and other vessels used for ceremonial purposes. But there the comparison ends. Instead of encouraging virtue these murals and mosaics portray the gods performing deeds of derring-do, behaving capriciously, or copulating with naughty nymphs. They say that you can tell the species of a tree by the type of fruit it produces. What a shame that the fruit the Roman society produced was that of violence, greed and cruelty on a scale that the world had not seen before.

Vindolanda means Chesterholm or Little Chester and it is here that the answer is found to our curry mystery. In 2005 an archaeological dig by English Heritage in Chester unearthed evidence of a 3rd century chicken curry, outside a Roman amphitheatre. I kid you not! Not only that but it was in a little disposable pot. In other words it was probably the first ever takeaway!

It is known that the Romans brought coriander to Britain so why not other spices? The Eastern Roman Empire included Mesopotamia, formerly the kingdom of Sumer, an area covered by parts of modern Iran and Iraq. Ancient Sumerian inscriptions were found recently which gave a recipe for curry, dating back to around 1700 BC. Therefore, chicken curry in Roman

Britain is not so surprising because some Roman soldiers probably came from Africa and the Middle East!

Now there's a thought.

Chapter 22
Valhalla and the 'Pipe-Clenchers'

Said Odin, "I cleared Valhalla
For coming of slain men.
Here to me I expect
Heroes coming from the world"
- 'The Poetic Edda'

The sun was shining. The wind was blowing in my face, making my hair stream behind me. The horse beneath me gave a sudden surge and powered forward at great speed, hooves thundering on the springy turf. At my call a great cry went up from all the many horsemen at my side and, as one, they spurred their steeds forward for the chase.

The plateau of High Street Fell lay before me, a mile in length, and at the periphery of vision the great mountain Helvellyn soared majestically into the sky. It rose and fell in my sight as the great black horse accelerated, and then steadied as we reached the gallop. At my back the other riders faded from the race and I pulled up short to await them, my horse snorting and stamping with impatience.

Was I dreaming again? Was this some flashback to a Viking past life? Or was I to expect my sleeping wife with a glazed expression, about to strangle me? Actually no - the scene above forms one of the most powerful memories of my young teenage years. My friend Fred and I were on holiday in Pooley Bridge in the Lake District and we had been horse riding on the fells above Ullswater. About thirty boys attended this house party run by Scripture Union at Barton House, where we stayed in dormitories, listened to Bible talks and engaged in lots of fun activities. In addition to horse riding we climbed some mighty peaks and canoed on Ullswater. Boys and leaders came from all parts of the country for this holiday, although Fred and I tended to mope around together for most of the time.

It was at this ramshackle and comfortable old house that I came across my first old Rover, which belonged to an equally ramshackle and comfortable chap called Mr Reading, who was the holiday leader. He was a true eccentric and Fred still has a photo of him somewhere wearing a knotted hanky on his head and his trousers rolled up to the knees. He is paddling about in Ullswater with a fishing net, like some middle-class version of Monty Python's 'Gumby'.

Speaking of class this was the first time I was laughed at for using northern dialect. Two girls of about sixteen were helping in the kitchens and were handing out duties to the boys, such as clearing the tables. I had been allocated the job of drying the dishes, so I politely asked these two teenage matrons if I could borrow a 'pot' towel. Well, you would think that I had dropped my trousers and stood on a bucket to recite nonsense verse. The two looked incredulous.

"A '*pot*' towel… oh, you mean a '*tea*' towel?" and they collapsed into paroxysms of giggles and shared looks.

I was miserable. My youthful fantasies about them were not the same after that.

Nevertheless this was the only slight cloud on the horizon and I really enjoyed these holidays, which Fred and I attended every summer for several years. They introduced us to the Christian faith and taught us some prayers so that we wouldn't have to be heathens anymore which, in my opinion, was a jolly good thing!

This was also my introduction to the Lake District and it was love at first sight. My paltry prose can only fail to do justice to its splendour, but I shall do my best. These childhood memories were coming to the fore because today we were lodging at Pooley Bridge in the northeast of the Lake District, after travelling down from Hadrian's Wall. We had come via the lovely-sounding Eden Valley, a place where you can still find red squirrels and so, carefully avoiding squirrels, we were now approaching what must be the 'jewel in the crown' of Pennine beauty and grandeur.

When the scenery becomes lovely and the road broad and quiet then 'Auntie' comes into her own. This is the sort of life she was made for, with the route rolling and twisting gently and other motor cars few and far between. It was time to switch on the valve radio, which is permanently tuned to Radio 4 Long Wave, and listen to my favourite comedy quiz show.

The aim was to meander south and west, ending up at Ravenglass on the west coast, staying at wayside inns or B & B's en route. We could then be said to have completed our idiosyncratic trail around the Pennines. For the world-weary traveller here indeed is Valhalla, a place of peace and balm for the 21st century urban warrior. When the great peaks of Blencathra and Skiddaw appear on the horizon I feel as though I am coming home and 'Auntie' speeds up to carry us over from one world to the next - the glorious Lake District.

We headed along the side of Ullswater, with High Street on the far shore dwarfing the little steamers that ploughed up and down on the water. We decided to have a late picnic on one of the pebbly beaches and, as we ate our sandwiches, we gazed across the lake, marvelling at the abundance of flora surrounding it. On the shoreline were to be found twisted hawthorns, gnarled like old men, and beneath them bog orchid and sundew. On the lower slopes of High Street there were juniper bushes and all types of heather such as ling, bell-heather, bilberry and crowberry. In the wet gullies below could be seen various herbs, with wonderful names like wood cranesbill, wild angelica and roseroot, and (the practically unbeatable) fleabane and sneezewort; all this in addition to Wordsworth's famous daffodils.

Although the daffodils were out there were still 'snow bones' on the mountains and it promised to be a chilly night. By the time we had finished our leisurely meal and Meg had chased sticks into the lake, it was almost twilight. Despite this we thought it would be nice to have a look at Aira Force waterfall, which was close by the shore, and so we headed up the path towards the distant sound of falling water. The climb was steep, through thick woods but eventually we reached the falls.

Aira Force is a sizeable body of water and just now it was in full spate. It plunged over a crag high above and thundered into a basin at our feet that formed a natural grotto. This would have been impressive enough but what made it really special was that someone had had a bonfire and the dying flames and embers suffused the whole grotto with reddy-orange light. The foam from Aira Force refracted the glow into a thousand jewels of yellow, orange and red, ever changing. The sparks flew upwards into what was by now a completely clear night sky. There was no light pollution here, except from the fire, and the endless stars twinkled back at us, white against the colours of the misty falls. I expected Valhalla to appear at any minute.

There was nothing particularly paradisiacal about the B & B we were staying in that night in Pooley Bridge, or at least about one of the other guests. As soon as he saw our dog this American guy started telling us some grisly story about how he had once killed a dog with his bare hands and what is the best way to do it. However, this disturbing encounter was made up for in part by the fact that they were selling 'Jennings' beer at £1 per pint in the local pub.

Next day we took the road to Glenridding, at the southern end of Ullswater. Although you can hire boats at Glenridding you might decide you want to go mountain climbing rather than sailing, because a very big mountain can be found here – Helvellyn, which fills up completely the space between Ullswater and Thirlmere. Helvellyn rises to a height of 3,117 ft, making it the third highest mountain in England, but take thought before you ascend the broad path to the summit; like any proper mountain Helvellyn should not be undertaken lightly. This fell is not the subject for an afternoon stroll - it takes all day to get to the top and down again and you should have some climbing experience. The weather can change from sunshine, to snow, to fog, in a matter of minutes, and it features such delights as Striding Edge, which is a narrow path with a 1,000 ft drop on either side of it, and helpful signs telling how such-and-such a body plunged to their death at a certain spot.

One winter I took part in a course called 'Safety in the Hills' where the importance of having the correct clothing, maps and emergency rations before attempting a mountain ascent was impressed on us by the professionals in charge. We hiked up Helvellyn, bristling with equipment, but halfway up the weather closed in and it started to snow. The snowstorm quickly became a blizzard and we had to take shelter beneath a rock corrie but I felt safe with the professional climbers, who could probably have survived for a month up there if necessary. We were just settling down for the night when a figure loomed out of the snow, looking for all the world like a yeti. When it reached us this snow-covered apparition brushed itself off to reveal a man. He was wearing a mackintosh and wellington boots and holding a plastic carrier bag. His hair was plastered to his head and his extremities were all drooping under the weight of snow they had gathered. He looked anxiously at our astonished group and asked

"Is the café open on the top?"

There is lots of help available these days for the speculative climber of Helvellyn. For example, there is a well-equipped climbing centre at Glenridding, where you can find maps, routes, video tours and a massive range of cagoules, plus Kendal Mint Cake to fortify you. There are people on hand to advise you and dozens of walkers, runners and climbers who will be accompanying you to the top, along a well-beaten path. Despite this, I am not saying that it is easy. Helvellyn is still a big mountain by British standards and, just like the sea, it should be treated with respect.

The last word on fell walking has to go to the Coniston Tigers. They were a climbing club formed by Harry Griffin in the 1930s, based in Coniston. They were named after the adventurous European mountaineers who explored the Himalayas and who were called 'the tigers of the snow' by their Sherpa bearers. Harry was a local boy who wrote extensively about the Lakeland fells in The Guardian's 'Country Diary', over a period of 53 years, which only ended with his death in 2004 at the age of 93.

They were fearless folk 'The Tigers', who would think nothing of ascending a 600 foot rock gully in winter in order to skate on a frozen tarn. Looking at some of the photographs in his book 'The Coniston Tigers', you have to admire the indomitable spirit of these men and women. One of my favourites is of a row of anoraks stood stiffly in the snow as if on a washing line, frozen solid. Another is of Harry's wife, Mollie, being used as a 'patient' in a mountain rescue exercise. She is shown being hauled at 90 degrees up a sheer rock face, with members of the Coniston Tigers belaying her out, all of them perched at impossible angles on the cliff. None of them seem particularly concerned, not even Mollie, although it's difficult to tell with her as she is strapped onto a stretcher. An additional pleasingly eccentric touch is that they are all clenching pipes tightly between their teeth, probably even Mollie. Goodness knows what would have happened if one of them had had to relight it.

Harry described the lure of the mountains as well as anybody I have read when he wrote:

"You can still find places, hundreds of places if you know where to look, where you can be alone with your thoughts, and the little movements and sounds of the countryside."

Jane and I weren't for climbing today so we drove through Glenridding and over the Kirkstone Pass before taking the Hawkshead road out of Ambleside.

I really feel as though I am standing on the shoulders of giants when talking about the Lake District. How can one compete with Wordsworth and his daffodils, or Ruskin with his description of the view from his house overlooking Coniston? Then there is the other great Lake District literary giant - Beatrix Potter. She lived close to the delightful village of Hawkshead on the east side of Windermere, and it was here that she drew inspiration for Peter Rabbit, Mrs Tiggiwinkle and so on. Many shops in the village sell paraphernalia relating to Beatrix Potter. It is very easy to find them should you wish to, just make for the giant cardboard cut-out of a fluffy bunny.

There are other places of note in Hawkshead such as the Old Grammar School where you can see the graffiti etched by young William Wordsworth on a desk. The school is a museum these days and Jane and I decided to take a look round it. It is laid out like an old-fashioned schoolroom with a teacher's desk, a cane or two, some old books, slates and inkwells and so on. What we didn't anticipate, however, was some actor prancing up and down in a cap and gown brandishing one of the canes.

We should have read the small print before we went in because no sooner had we set foot over the doorstep than this over-enthusiastic thespian, behaving like Wackford Squeers, launched into some pre-prepared speech about us being late, accompanied by a mighty thwack of his cane on a table. Trying to grasp what was happening I glanced around the darkened room and could just make out several pairs of frightened eyes staring in mortal dread at our Lawrence Olivier of the classroom. They were other tourists who, like us, had been lured in here and were now trapped.

Obviously, this was supposed to be some sort of re-enactment of life in a 19th century school but I didn't really feel up to this particular type of reality game-show, and Jane was frankly terrified. The Method trained actor was really getting into his role. He chased us to a desk and then fulminated about the evils of 'tardiness' and the virtues of punctuality. All the time he was whacking desks with his cane, which was starting to look a bit frayed. Any minute now he was going to hurl a board-rubber at me, I just knew it.

Thankfully, after several minutes of sitting up straight and looking to the front, whilst the erstwhile schoolmaster talked about grammar and the British

Empire, a bell rang. I hadn't noticed another figure lurking in a dark corner of the room who now stepped forward with a hand bell. It was a frail and mousy-looking lady who looked as though she might once have been a tourist like us. She had obviously been ensnared at some time in the past and now lived and worked here, existing on crusts and charitable donations. Our antagonist glowered at the poor woman, who had had the temerity to interrupt him in mid-flow, and reluctantly dismissed us. I have never seen such a rush for the exit in my life. Jane wasn't herself for days.

That night we were staying in my favourite pub in Hawkshead, 'The King's Head'. It is a comely old place possessing all the ingredients necessary for a proper pub, such as a real fire, settles, intimate rooms and old farmers. We were just settling in at the bar when who should walk in but Nick Robinson, the BBC's Political Editor. He looked a little sheepish coming into the bar, as if he wasn't sure whether he would be recognised and whether, if he were, he would be happy about it. Nick grew up in the North, not far from where I did, but he hides it well. Maybe he had come to visit BBC ex-colleague Alex Brodie, who is a fellow Northerner and who left the 'beeb' to start the splendid 'Hawkshead Brewery'.

If you are ever this far south in the Lake District and like a bit of an adventure then you must take a trip to Piel Island. Naturally, you have to phone the king first. Piel has a king you see. The kingdom began with the last German invasion of England (more of which later!).

You can drive to Piel Island at lowtide but it is not recommended, because of the quicksand. There are soft sands south of Barrow, on the northerly tip of Morecambe Bay. The day I phoned the king he wasn't keen on us visiting because the tides weren't favourable, but he changed his mind after chatting for a few moments.

"I'm here on the island alone," he said, "it can get lonely."

He told us to meet him at the causeway that leads from the mainland and so, promptly, we arrived an hour later. The King was just pulling up in his Landrover. I didn't know whether to shake hands with him or bow the knee so I waited to see what he was like.

He turned out to be a very nice chap, and talkative, probably because he was on his own. I wanted to find out why he was a king. Apparently the tradition goes back to 1487 when a Yorkist priest named Symonds noticed that a pupil of his - Lambert Simnel, bore an uncanny resemblance to the son of Edward IV. Symonds determined to use Simnel as the figurehead for an invasion of England, in order to dethrone the Lancastrian Henry VII and re-establish the Yorkist line. With a ragged army of Irish and German mercenaries Symonds and Simnel started their invasion on Piel Island. Simnel was crowned king there and then the whole army proceeded to march overland towards

London. They were eventually defeated in a battle near Stoke.

These days the kingdom is confined to the island and its duties and powers are entirely ceremonial. Rather prosaically the island now comes under the jurisdiction of Barrow-in-Furness Urban District Council.

The king had to curtail his history lesson because the Land Rover suddenly plunged into the sea. I hadn't really expected this. I thought that the causeway went all the way across to the island, but not so. We found ourselves bonnet-deep in seawater, wallowing away from the shore. In such situations one tends to trust the experienced professional but in this case I became a little nervous when he kept stopping the car and getting out to test the depth of the water and the firmness of the seabed.

I needn't have worried because we were soon making an amphibious-type landing on the island. The kingdom of Piel is not very big – no more than a few acres. It consists of tough, windblown, tufty grass surrounded by pebbly beach. The main feature is a castle or 'Peel', hence the name, built to guard the port and Abbey of Furness, in the 14th century. It is a ruin now, which is not surprising considering its turbulent past. By turns the island has been used for invasion plots, smuggling and piracy as well as more legitimate purposes. The Vikings used this spot as a lighthouse or rather a fire-house to warn of shallow waters.

The king still has a crowning ceremony but he doesn't have to be the son of the previous king, you can apply for the post. In 2006 there were hundreds of applicants for the job. If you fail to become king you can always try to get a knighthood by doing some good deed. I offered to round up his sheep with Meg but the king wasn't impressed.

The other main building on the island is the pub, 'The Ship Inn'. When we visited it was being refurbished and so we had to have a drink in a little shed set up temporarily as a replacement. The king gets to run the pub as part of his job but I wondered how many customers he got. He said that it was fairly busy in summer but tended to be somewhat deserted in winter. An 1813 account by a visitor tells a similar story. He recounts that the landlord confessed to 'comforting himself with his beer barrel' at such times. I like my solitude but I think you have to be a special sort to be the king here. Wordsworth's poems seem to indicate that he liked solitude. He wrote a poem about Piel called 'Rampside', which is the name of the little community on the mainland nearest to Piel. Here is a short extract:

'I was thy neighbour once thou rugged Pile!
Four summer weeks I dwelt in sight of thee:
I saw thee every day, and all the while,
Thy form was sleeping on a glassy sea'.

I prefer his 'Daffodils'.

A challenge of a different sort awaited us next day. We had decided to drive over the Wrynose Pass and the Hardknott Pass. They said it couldn't be done. They said I was mad, but I figured that driving up a mountain couldn't be so bad. However, as I came to discover, the Hardknott Pass and the Wrynose Pass, between Elterwater and Wastwater, should have health warnings on them. Beware! They are not for the faint-hearted driver. These are evil ways for the inexperienced - practically vertical and twisted like a corkscrew. Not only that but the road is narrow, with a high camber in the middle. They will test even a modern car, never mind such as 'Auntie'. I have a friend who has travelled roads all over the Alps and when I mentioned the Wrynose Pass he became grave.

"It's worse than the Tourmalet," he said, his shaking hand reaching for the whisky.

Actually, they do have health warnings at the foot of each of the passes. There are at least five signs that tell you to take extreme care and not to bother at all in winter; in fact that you must be mad to attempt it in any weather! We did manage it but afterwards I was so traumatised that I followed a convoy of cars into the pub at the bottom, where we all sat looking at each other with wild eyes, saying nothing. I hadn't dared to stop halfway up but I did feel a bit sorry for the two old ladies in a Morris Minor who were standing by their immobile car looking slightly shocked. I hope somebody rescued them.

On the far side of the Wrynose and Hardknott passes is the village of Boot, and it was this particular piece of paradise that was spoiled, temporarily, one summer's day in 2010. For it was here that local man Derrick Bird shot himself, after going on a killing spree that left twelve people dead and eleven injured. The killings all took place in the coastal area, centred around the town of Whitehaven. The victims included Bird's twin brother, David, his solicitor, a fellow taxi-driver and several apparently random people - pedestrians, drivers and a mole-catcher at work in a nearby field. Bird then committed suicide in Boot. What was motivating the man? How had things become so desperate? At what point did evil overcome him? Was it a quick process or a slow one, the build up of years of bitterness, resentment and disappointment? It seems that in this world no place is paradise. Wasn't it Milton who said that 'the mind can make a heaven out of hell or a hell out of heaven'?

Thankfully, on the day we drove through there were no clouds in the sky, literally or metaphorically, for we were heading to Wasdale, site of England's highest mountain, deepest lake and smallest Anglican Church. The air was quite still as we drove alongside Wastwater, so that we could see a perfect reflection of Scafell Pike and Kirk Fell in its glassy surface.

The road is a dead end, finishing at 'The Wasdale Head Inn' and St Olaf's Church. The church is genuinely tiny but well worth a look. It is named after a Viking king and saint, Olaf Haraldsson, who lived in the late 10th and early 11th centuries and died in battle. There are further connections between the church and the Vikings because the fields around it are remembered as 'The Viking Fields' and, more excitingly, the cruck beams and trusses of the church are thought to be made from the timbers of Viking longships.

On a stained glass window behind the altar an inscription reads,

'I raise my eyes unto the hills, from whence cometh my strength'.

The Wasdale Head Inn has been the headquarters of English climbing for well over 100 years. But this doesn't mean it is uncivilised. There is a lovely oak-panelled dining room serving imaginative cuisine, and bedrooms with views to take your breath away. In the bar you will inevitably meet many climbers and hikers and we got to know a great character who called himself Stumbling Dave. Dave loved walking the fells but his problem was that he suffered from cerebral palsy. It wasn't so severe that it stopped him climbing and rambling but it did make him stumble a lot. He told us that every day when he stayed here, prior to going on the mountains he would take a walk around the cemetery of St Olaf's Church and look at the gravestones of the many climbers who had died in accidents. It always made him more careful, he said.

From the Boot end of Wasdale you can catch a miniature steam railway to Ravenglass. It used to transport iron ore but these days it just transports happy tourists to the most westerly point of the Lakes. Ravenglass was a thriving Roman port and marked the very end of the defensive structures that culminated in

Hadrian's Wall. It once had a garrison of 500 men but the only remains of it now are at Muncaster Castle where you can find the ruins of a Roman bath-house.

Ravenglass is a quiet and charming little place, with a number of holiday homes leading down on to the beach. As they are not always occupied this gives it a slightly melancholy air. Perhaps Ravenglass feels a tad wistful about the fact that it is sited in the shadows of mighty Scafell and Great Gable.

I feel a bit that way myself as I reach the end of my personal tour of the Pennines. It has been a journey redolent with memories, mostly happy and good but with some sombre thoughts as well. Have I 'found myself', or the Viking within? They say that when the Vikings went into battle they followed a three point plan. Firstly, they would find some high ground on which they could look down on their enemies. When the battle commenced they would charge down and engage the enemy as fiercely and quickly as possible; this was the onset. The last part of the plan was to withdraw, back up the hill, before the element of surprise was lost and they could be struck down.

So, when life makes you metaphorically withdraw up a hill, backwards, regard it as a merely tactical retreat and a strategy for ultimate success.

The Vikings set off in little boats to see the world but one place they stopped and settled in was Northern England. As I look back over Scafell I reflect on the pleasure and peace I have obtained from the hills and the mountains. I know that they can't sort out all life's problems but I am reminded of that inscription again from the church in Wasdale Head: 'I raise my eyes unto the hills, from whence cometh my help'.

Actually that is only part of the verse and not quite correct – it should read:

'I raise my eyes unto the hills; from whence does my help come? It comes from The Lord, who made heaven and earth.' (Psalm 121 vs. 1)

You will have to make up your own mind for, as the Viking saying goes, 'One man's tale is but half a tale'.

I walk down to the beach and look out across the Irish Sea at a majestic sunset, and I throw a few pebbles for Meg into the gently lapping tide. Just then I sense an arm link mine as I brood and Jane smiles at me.

"I don't think you are all Viking," she says. "You're not really an alpha mayo." I am tempted to look round for an aggressive salad dressing, but I realise that she means 'alpha male'.

We turn and walk back to catch the little train that will return us to Eskdale and Wasdale, where 'Auntie' is waiting to take us home. Meg follows, watching us closely, the sun casting a long shadow behind her.

Shadows

I miss you still,
Lying by the door,
Forever looking back at me.
The space is empty now.
I miss you still,
Running and jumping on the hills,
Watching for a sign from me.
The hill is empty now.
I miss you still,
Lying on the window sill,
Waiting all the long day for me.
Cut flowers there now.
I see you yet,
As I let go your leash,
And a stranger leads you away.
Only a shadow now.

'Sheepdog' – by Peter Brook

Appendix I
Northern Stereotypes

(When you observe a northern stereotype in this book please tick below, adding a page reference.)

1.   Loud - gives strong opinions; lacking tact.
2.   Stupid - innately lacking intelligence.
3.   Ignorant - lacking knowledge; often linked with 2.
4.   Uncivilised – scant control of bodily functions
5.   Boorish - see 'Loud'
6.   Lacking taste - eats tripe
7.   Unfashionable – flat cap, raincoat, whippet
8.   Unhealthy - diet of pies and mushy peas
9.   Miserly – prefaces payment with "How much!" (see cheap)
10.   Crude - rude and inarticulate
11.   Porky or toilet-based sense of humour
12.   Wet through - due to rain
13.   Likes beer – as opposed to wine
14.   Cheap (see miserly)

Appendix II
Some Pennine Sayings

'It'll stick to your ribs two years after you're dead' (good, solid food)

'He'll eat you out of house and home' (a greedy person)

'Like a fart in a colander' (indecisive). This was also used in the forces in WWII.

'Stuck up like a piece of burnt leather' (someone snobbish)

'I'll go to the foot of our stairs' (an expression of shock and surprise)

'Eeh by gum' ('By God')

'You make a better door than a window' (on getting in the way)

'We're short of nothing that we've got' (an ironic comment on being poor)

'You can't get good ones under' (an ironic comment on goods of a poor quality)

'A scoddy effort' (something small or of poor quality)

'Stand and stare back' (a nonsensical reply to a rude question)

'Bestolukannofiddlin' (look but don't touch)

'Frozzen daft' (very cold)

'Put wood int t'hole' (shut the door)

'Put some coyle (coal) on' (get a move on)

'Faffing about' (messing around wasting time)

'Who's she – the cat's mother?' (A reprimand for speaking disrespectfully to Mum)

'As black as Dick's hat-band' (a stormy or gloomy sky)

'It's stottin down' (raining hard)

'You'll catch something you'll never get rid of' (a warning about the dangers of not washing one's hands)

Appendix III
The Old Rover
(Sung to the tune of 'Wild Rover')

I drove an old Rover for many a year,
And I spent all my money on petrol and gear.
And now I'm returning it back to the store
And I never will drive the old Rover no more

And it's no, nay, never,
No nay never no more,
Will I drive the old Rover,
No never, no more.

I drove to the garage I used to frequent,
And I told the mechanic my money was spent.
I asked him for credit, he answered me nay,
Such a custom as yours I could have any day.

And it's no, nay, never,
No nay never, no more,
Will I drive the old Rover,
No never, no more.

A big starting handle I took from my side,
And I threatened to brain him if work was denied.
I said 'Get your spanners and tools out my friend,

I expect you to tackle and mend my Big End.

And it's no, nay, never,
No nay never, no more,
Will I drive the old Rover,
No never, no more.

I'll go home to my parents, and confess what I've done.
And I'll ask them to pardon their prodigal son.
And if they forgive me as oft-times before,
Sure I never will drive the old Rover no more.

And it's no, nay, never,
No nay never, no more,
Will I drive the old Rover,
No never, no more.

Odd Odes

Pickled Eggs

(After 'Balloons' by Sylvia Plath - who hated Whitby)

Since Christmas they have lived with us,
Tasty and white,
Oval egg shapes,
Taking up half the space,
In the pickle jar, not the bell jar.
Because that would leak,
Onto
The floor.

Going squelch and plop,
When attacked with a pickle fork.
Yellow ochre and brown vinegar
Spill.
My friend is making his egg,
Repeat like the wind,
Seeming to see a funny side to it.
He bites again,
Then sits, back,
Fat tum,
Contemplating a glass as clear,
As water.
A fiver in a grubby fist.
His round.

Ode to an Un-reconstituted Northerner

I await civilisation.

Two-Seater

(After Rampside by William Wordsworth)

I was thy neighbour once thou piece of art!
Four lonely hours I spent sitting on thee:
What happy thoughts pervade my heart
As here I sit and merely sigh,
For one true love to share my part.
So join me love as here we sit
Together now above the pit,
The Bronco beckons, strong and hard,
I left it there, beyond the yard.

Appendix IV
'Auntie's' Undies

The P4 was the first newly designed post-war Rover and production began in 1949 at the company's plant in Solihull. It coincided with the successful launch of the Land Rover in 1948 and the two vehicles spearheaded a 'golden age' for Rover, which continued throughout the 1950s and 60s. There were several incarnations of the P4, starting with the 60 and then, moving up numerically, the 75, 80, 90, 95, 100, 105 and 110. Each version reflected changing tastes in styling as well as advances in engineering, such as the addition of disc brakes from 1959 onwards, or electric windscreen washers.

The earlier models used aluminium sheeting in the panels but this was changed to steel on the 95 and 110 because of cost considerations. This increased the weight of the car and a fully laden 110 was approaching the two ton mark. The 8-gauge steel and mighty chassis made the P4 a formidable beast and tales of its strength are legendary. One old Rover owner told me, rather sadly, that he was selling his automatic version because he felt it was a danger. He had parked at the shops one day, just to post a letter, and had left the engine running. He put the handbrake on, and leaving the car (as he thought) in neutral, he locked the door and walked off. Unfortunately, he had left the car in 'Drive' which meant that it began to creep forward very slowly, despite the handbrake. The first thing it hit was a British Leyland Ambassador, which it squashed both completely and effortlessly. The noise brought the poor owner running back but in his panic he could not get the door of the rogue Rover undone. The next obstacle to this juggernaut was a set of concrete posts designed to protect pedestrians doing their shopping. These were chopped down as neatly and cleanly as a combine harvester going through a field of hay and then on she went, quietly but relentlessly, across the shopping parade before finally coming to rest halfway through a branch of the National Westminster Bank.

"The irony is," continued the former owner with a sigh, "that despite the thousands of pounds worth of damage to another vehicle, council property and the bank, my Rover only required fairly minor repairs to its front end."

The mighty engine unit driving the P4 reached its peak of power with the 110. This engine was a 'straight six' cylinder, bored out to achieve 123 brake horsepower, or 2625cc, which made it almost a match for the MGB sports car. However, the Rover was far too civilised to engage in unseemly battles off the mark and she really aimed at smooth and steady acceleration. Mechanics used to say that the P4 was never tuned properly until you could stand a threepenny bit on the cylinder head whilst the engine was idling, thus effecting a seemingly effortless transmission of power.

I do remember that a Rover P4 was only one of two cars (the other being a Jaguar) that my friend's Triumph Bonneville motorbike couldn't keep up with on a long journey down to London on the M6. His bike was fast but difficult to handle at speeds of over 100 mph for any length of time.

The P4 tended to attract a certain type of driver. In the 1950s it was standard issue for Bishops and Bank Managers and it also graced the car parks of Whitehall. Aficionados christened her 'Auntie' but carping critics dubbed her 'the hippo' or 'the poor man's Rolls Royce'. Later on, after she had been cast aside by progress, the P4 became a favourite for steady, practical, pipe-smoking individuals, who always waved sombrely to each other when passing on the roads. I was unusual when I became a P4 owner because, although I did smoke a pipe, I was only twenty years old. Indeed one old chap refused to sell me his car because he thought I was too young.

"When I find the right person," he informed me gravely, "I will *give* the car to him."

It is this sort of affection that 'Auntie' generates amongst her followers. Why don't you consider buying one? They are free to tax, cheap to insure and have an enthusiastic band of supporters who beat the AA 'into a cocked hat' when it comes to help and rescue. Alright, the car only achieves twenty miles to the gallon and the two-gallon oil sump takes a pint of 'Duckhams' every week, but you will be entering a rare and civilised world of calm and quietude, unless you have to use the starting handle!